PLANTS OF THE ROCKY MOUNTAINS

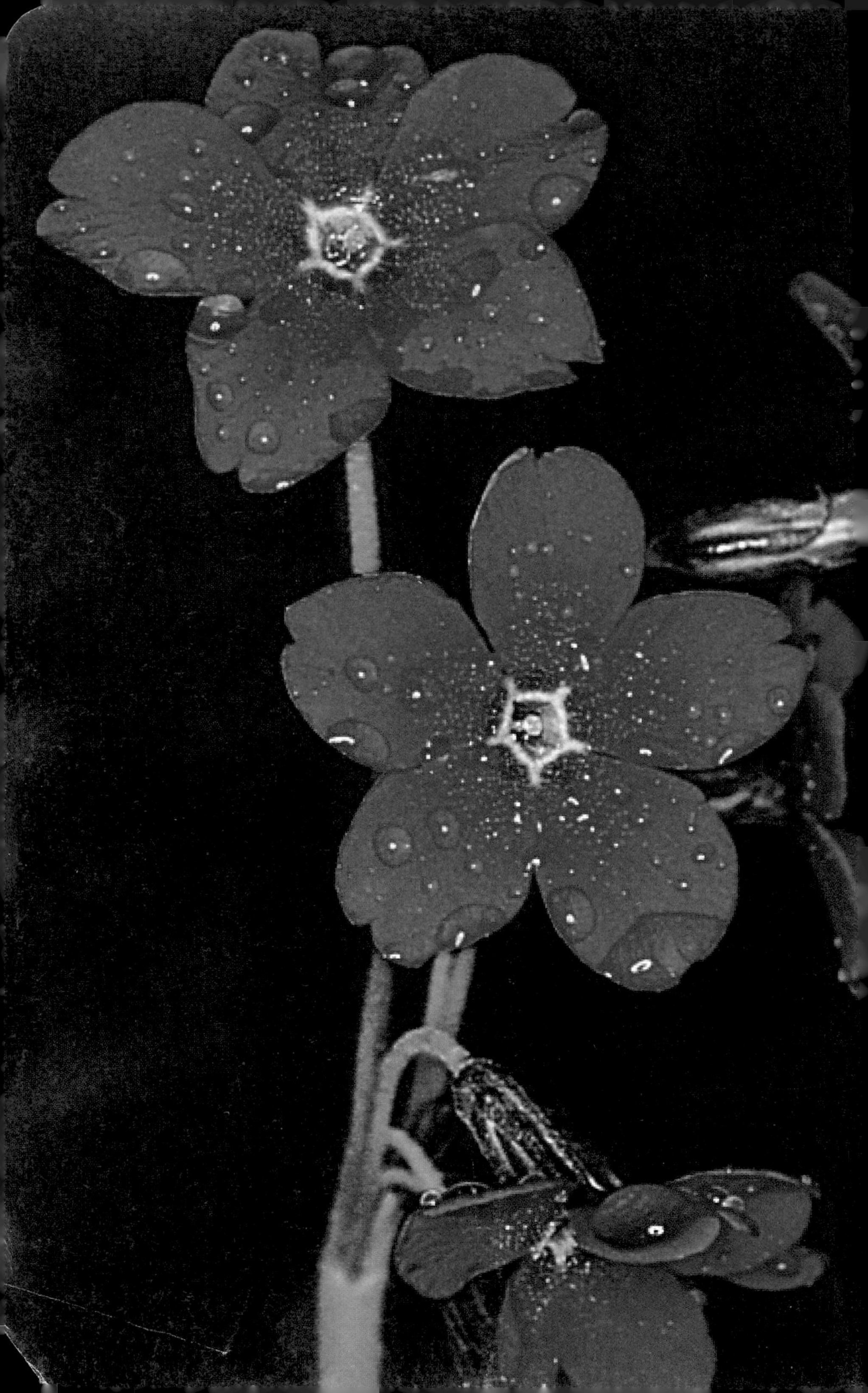

PLANTS OF THE ROCKY MOUNTAINS

LINDA KERSHAW

ANDY MacKINNON

JIM POJAR

First printed in 1998 10 9 8 7 6 5 4
Printed in Canada

The Publisher: **Lone Pine Publishing**

#206, 10426-81 Avenue
Edmonton, AB T6E 1X5
Canada

202A 1110 Seymour Street
Vancouver, BC V6B 3N3
Canada

1901 Raymond Ave., SW, Suite C
Renton, WA 98055
USA

Lone Pine Publishing website:
http://www.lonepinepublishing.com

Canadian Cataloguing in Publication Data

Kershaw, Linda J., 1951–
Plants of the Rocky Mountains

Includes bibliographical references and index.
ISBN 1-55105-088-9

1. Mountain plants—Rocky Mountains—Identification.
2. Botany—Rocky Mountains. I. MacKinnon, A. (Andrew), 1956–
II. Pojar, Jim, 1948– III. Title.
QK139.K47 1998 581.978 C97-910595-1

Senior Editor: Nancy Foulds
Project Editor: Lee Craig
Editorial: Lee Craig, Erin McCloskey, Heather Markham
Production Management: David Dodge, Gregory Brown
Production Manager: David Dodge
Design and Layout: Bruce Timothy Keith, Gregory Brown, Federico Caceres
Maps: Volker Bodegom
Cover Design: Gregory Brown
Cover Photo: Daryl Benson
Separations and Film: Elite Lithographers, Edmonton, Alberta, Canada
Printing: Quality Color Press Inc., Edmonton, Alberta, Canada

The publisher gratefully acknowledges the support of the Department of Canadian Heritage.

Funding for this publication was provided in part by the Canadian Forest Service.

CONTENTS

LIST OF KEYS AND ILLUSTRATIONS

Keys

Illustrations

ACKNOWLEDGEMENTS

We'd like to thank some of the people who helped produce this book. Trevor Goward wrote the lichens section, and the bryophytes section was written by René Belland and Dale Vitt. Paul Alaback provided information for the introduction.

Many people took the photos used in this guide. They include Lorna Allen, Gerry Allen, the BC Ministry of Forests, BC Parks, Laird Blackwell, Frank Boas, Robin Bovey, Joan Burbridge, Adolf Ceska, Brenda Chambers, Ray Coupé, R. Blake Dickens, Robert Frisch, Joyce Gould, Leslie Hill, Julie Hrapko, Alex Ilsenberg, Derek Johnson, the Kamloops Forest Region, Linda Kershaw, Dennis Lloyd, Ron Long, Robin Love, Ches Lyons, Bill Merilees, Bob Norton, Jim Pojar, George Powell, Dave Ralph, Anna Roberts, Martin Ross, Rob Scagel, Carol Thompson, Nancy and Robert Turner, Dale Vitt, L.K. Wade, Rob Walker, Pat Warrington, Mike Wheatley, George Whitehead, Brian Wikeem, Dave Williams, Karen Vail, Joe Duft, D. Strickler and John Worrall. Photo credits are listed on page 365.

Line drawings have been used from Britton, N. and A. Brown. (1913), and with kind permission from the British Columbia Forest Service, the Royal British Columbia Museum (G.W. Douglas, 1982 and 1995), Linda Kershaw, Trevor Goward (Goward et. al., 1994) and the University of Washington Press (C.L. Hitchcock et. al., 1955–69). Line drawing credits are listed on page 366.

We would also like to acknowledge the contribution of the editors and contributors of 4 previous publications, which provide continuity to this book: *Plants of Northern British Columbia* (including Ray Coupé, George Argus, Frank Boas, Craig DeLong, George Douglas, Trevor Goward, Andy MacKinnon, Jim Pojar, Rosamond Pojar and Anna Roberts; 1992); *Plants of Coastal British Columbia* (including Paul Alaback, Joe Antos, Trevor Goward, Ken Lertzmann, Andy MacKinnon, Jim Pojar, Rosamund Pojar, Andrew Reed, Nancy Turner and Dale Vitt; 1994); *Plants of the Western Boreal Forest and Aspen Parkland* (including Trevor Goward, Derek Johnson, Linda Kershaw, Andy MacKinnon, Jim Pojar and Dale Vitt; 1995); and *Plants of Southern Interior British Columbia* (including Joe Antos, Ray Coupé, George Douglas, Rich Evans, Trevor Goward, Marianne Ignace, Dennis Lloyd, Roberta Parish, Rosamund Pojar and Anna Roberts; 1996).

Many thanks to the Lone Pine staff for their assistance in putting this guide together: Lee Craig, Heather Markham and Nancy Foulds edited the text; Erin McCloskey and Lee Craig helped to organize the photos and illustrations, and to illustrate the keys; Greg Brown and David Dodge co-ordinated production; Michelle Bynoe scanned the illustrations; Volker Bodegom produced the maps; and Bruce Keith, Federico Caceres and Greg Brown did the final layout. Special thanks to Lone Pine, and in particular Shane Kennedy, for giving us the opportunity to write this book, and for providing the logistical and financial support that made its production possible.

—Linda Kershaw, Andy MacKinnon & Jim Pojar

ABOUT THIS GUIDE

The Rocky Mountains contain some of North America's most scenic and ecologically diverse regions. With their snow-capped peaks, clear, sparkling lakes and vast expanses of wilderness, the Rockies are one of the world's most popular tourist destinations. Because of their unique natural features, many parks and reserves have been established (see map on inside back cover).

The Rocky Mountains do not recognize political boundaries; they span 2 countries and 11 states, provinces and territories. This guide presents information for the Rocky Mountains in general, an area defined ecologically rather than politically. It is designed for people interested in the plants that make up the forests, meadows, grasslands and wetlands that blanket the Rocky Mountains.

The Rocky Mountain region is a large, diverse area, rich in plant and animal species. This guide describes common and distinctive plants in the Rockies, including trees, shrubs, herbs, grasses, ferns, mosses and lichens. Although comprehensive, it does not include all of the 1,000s of plant species in the Rocky Mountains.

In most cases, plants are described in everyday language. If technical terms are used, they are defined in the glossary and/or explained in the introductions to the major plant groups, and many are also illustrated. Plants are illustrated with colour photos, and sometimes with line drawings to show the habit (the appearance of the whole plant) or small details that may help with identification. Keys are also included for some of the larger and more difficult groups, to help you recognize diagnostic characteristics used to identify different species. Most diagnostic characteristics in the keys can be observed with the naked eye (or sometimes with a 10x lens). Definite identification of species in some groups requires microscopic examination and/or consultation with more technical references, many of which are listed at the end of this book.

Metric measurements are used throughout the guide, but they are easily converted to the **Imperial system**. One kilometre equals 0.6 miles, so multiply the number of **kilometres** by 1.6 to estimate the distance in **miles**. One metre equals 3.3 feet, so triple the number of **metres** and add 10 percent to determine the length in **feet**. Also, temperature is given in Celsius degrees. You can almost double each **Celsius** degree when converting to **Fahrenheit** (the actual ratio is 1 : 1.8), but because 0° C equals 32° F, you must add 32 to the total to determine temperature.

HOW TO USE THIS GUIDE

The guide describes species from all of the major groups of plants in the Rocky Mountains. Similar species that might be confused with one another are grouped so they can be compared easily. Within each section, plants are organized by family, with similar families grouped together, and within each family similar genera and species are shown close together.

The quickest way to identify an unfamiliar plant is by browsing through this guide. First, take a careful look at the plant you want to identify. You might have to get down on your hands and knees, or find something to stand on. As a general rule, **bring your eye to the flower, don't bring the flower to your eye**. Don't pick wildflowers or break branches from trees and shrubs to have a closer look. Picking is against the law in many parts of the Rockies, and for good reason. Millions of people come to this region each year because of its natural beauty, and if each visitor took home a bouquet of wildflowers, there would soon be very few left to enjoy. Picking can eradicate some species.

Once you have had a good look at the plant, flip to the major group to which it belongs. For example, if it is a shrub, go to the shrub section. Sections are easily identified by the coloured bars at the top of each page. Now, browse through the photos and line drawings looking for a plant that closely resembles your specimen. The herbs section is the largest in the book, so a

colour key to the wildflowers has been included (pp. 83–89) to help you to find plants with similar colours of flowers. Once you think you have found your plant, read the description to see if it matches. Different characteristics are important for identification in different groups. For example, petal size and shape may be important characteristics in 1 group, and leaf characteristics may be diagnostic in another group. Key features are highlighted with bold text, so check them first. Most flowering plants in the Rockies change dramatically in appearance as the growing season advances, beginning with immature leaves and flower buds early in the growing season and ending with fruits and withering leaves in autumn. A '**General**' description of the plant, followed by more detailed accounts of its '**Leaves**,' '**Flowers**' and '**Fruits**,' should help you to identify a specimen at any time during this cycle. Some plants can change dramatically with changes in their environment. Plants belonging to the same species, but growing in different habitats, can have very different characteristics. For example, dandelions (*Taraxacum* spp., p. 220) in moist, shady sites may have large, spreading leaves and long flower stalks, but on a nearby trail or parking lot they may have short-stalked flowers nestled in flat-lying rosettes of small leaves. The size ranges included in the descriptions help to identify the variability you can expect. Plants also change dramatically as they grow and mature. The blooming period for each flowering plant is presented at the end of the 'Flowers' section. It indicates when to look for flowers, and indirectly, when you are more likely to find fruits. However, many plants are found over many elevations and latitudes, and their range of flowering times can be very broad. Plants on sheltered, south-facing slopes in the foothills may bloom in June, but the same species, growing in cold, exposed alpine regions, may not produce flowers until August.

The '**Where Found**' section describes the general habitat and distribution of the species. For example, if the habitat is described as 'dry, rocky, exposed ridges' and you are in a moist, shady forest, chances are you are looking at a different species. The general elevational zones, described next, include plains, foothills, montane, subalpine and alpine. The elevation of each of these zones varies with latitude, aspect and exposure (see Vegetation section, p. 14), but this information may also help you to confirm your identification. The third part of the 'Where Found' section describes the general **range** of the species **within the Rocky Mountains**. The range is defined using political regions (e.g., southern BC and Alberta to Colorado), and it is described **only** as it relates to the Rocky Mountains. Distribution notes can help you to verify your identification, or perhaps you will discover that you have found a new location for a plant.

Browsing can help you identify many plants, and it will usually help you recognize the group of species to which your specimen belongs. In some cases, however, especially when dealing with large, complex groups, it is important to recognize the key characteristics that separate 1 species (or genus) from another. Good diagnostic characteristics are fairly constant from 1 plant to the next. Consistency is more important than visibility, and such features are not always obvious at first glance. Dichotomous (2-branched) **keys**, based on diagnostic characteristics, are provided as a guide to identification for some of the larger and more perplexing groups. Each number in the keys presents 2 alternative descriptions for the same feature(s). You choose the description that best fits your plant, and then go to the next pair of choices (as indicated by the number at the end of the entry). When the entry ends with a name, you have made an identification, so you flip to that entry to check. Sometimes, you may find that important features are not present on your specimen. Careful examination may reveal features from other seasons (e.g., withered petals; dried fruits from the previous year), but it often requires an active imagination to reconstruct a lost fruit or flower.

The last section for each species is entitled '**Notes**.' It usually begins with descriptions of common plants that are similar to the main species along with general descriptions of their habitat and distribution. The 'Notes' section usually ends with general notes of interest.

Plant Names

Common and scientific names are given for each plant. Common names vary greatly from 1 region to the next, and most plants in this guide have several common names. The most widely used, or in some cases the most appropriate, common name(s) are presented for each species. Scientific names are generally more widely accepted, because they tend to be relatively stable and more clearly defined—a scientific name must be published in a scientific journal with justification for its adoption, whereas a common name evolves through everyday use. However, plant taxonomists often disagree, and species concepts and names change. Scientific names in this guide generally follow the *Flora of North America* (1993) and Kartesz (1994) for vascular plants, Anderson et al. (1990) for mosses and liverworts and Esslinger et al. (1995) for lichens. Other names recently applied to a species appear at the first of the 'Notes' section.

THE REGION

The Rocky Mountain chain is over 4,800 km long and about 400–550 km wide, encompassing the Brooks Range in Alaska and the Selwyn and Mackenzie mountains in the Yukon and NWT. Although many plants in the northern mountains are described here, the focus is on the region from northern BC (south of the Liard River) to New Mexico (north of Santa Fe). This area is generally divided into 3 main regions: 1. the Canadian Rockies; 2. the Northern US Rockies (sometimes subdivided into the Central or Middle Rockies and Northern Rockies); and 3. the Southern US Rockies. The Canadian Rockies extend from the Liard River in northern BC to the southern border of Glacier National Park in Montana, bounded by the plains in the east and the Rocky Mountain Trench in the west. The Rockies in northern Montana are often included in the Northern US Rockies, but ignoring political boundaries, these mountains are geologically and biologically a part of the Canadian Rockies. The abbreviations US, BC and NWT refer respectively to the United States, British Columbia and the Northwest Territories.

Geology and Landforms

The **Canadian Rockies** are composed mainly of sedimentary rocks, such as limestone and shale, which were laid down under an ancient sea up to 1.5 billion years ago. About 140 to 145 million years ago, 2 large plates in the earth's crust pushed up against each other, causing the surface layers of rock to ride upwards over the underlying or 'basement' rock, either folding (accordion-like) or breaking and thrusting upwards. The result was the Canadian Rockies. It is a relatively young landscape, recently sculpted by glaciers into deep, U-shaped valleys, steep slopes and high peaks. Several glaciers, covering about 300 sq km along the mountain crests, still remain, grinding away rock and clouding streams with fine rock powder known as 'glacial flour.' Some of the highest mountains in this region include Mt. Robson (3,954 m), Mt. Cleveland (3,190 m) and Mt. Smythe (2,990 m).

The Canadian Rockies are generally divided into 4 main sections from east to west: 1. the foothills—a 25–50 km wide strip of relatively low-elevation ridges; 2. the front ranges—a 20–50 km wide band of higher mountains (up to 110 km wide in the north), in which the rock layers (strata) generally dip to the southwest, with steep slopes to the northeast; 3. the main ranges—a 40–50 km wide strip containing the highest mountains, many of which are castle-like with steep sides all around; and 4. the western ranges—a 0–20 km wide strip of mountains in which the rock layers (strata) dip to the northeast, with steep slopes to the southwest. The main and western ranges do not extend into the southern and northern parts of the Canadian Rockies.

The **Northern US and Southern US Rockies** are physically and geologically very different from the Canadian Rockies. The mountains are spread out into several small, parallel mountain chains. Many mountains are volcanic in origin, and those that are not are generally composed of metamorphic and igneous rocks (e.g., gneiss and granite), the material that makes up the continental plate ('basement' rock) underlying the Canadian Rockies. The US Rockies were created, in large part, by faults in the basement rock, rather than by folding of the upper rock layers. The raised sedimentary layers overlying the upthrust sections were worn away by erosion, exposing the underlying rock. In other cases, faulting brought magma to the surface in volcanoes and lava flows, which produced new landforms. Although the US Rockies are generally higher than Canadian Rockies, local relief is typically less (i.e., mountains are shorter from base to summit) because valley bottoms are high to begin with. Also, the US Rockies tend to be less obviously affected by glaciation, with fewer deep, U-shaped valleys or freshly cut mountain peaks.

The **Northern US Rockies** extend from Montana and Idaho to the Wind River and Salt River Ranges in Wyoming. They are bounded by the Great Plains on the east and by the Columbia Plateau and Great Basin on the west. Volcanic activity has been a major force in the formation of the Northern US Rockies. It has generally been associated with the westward movement of the continental plate over a 'hot spot'—a thin part of the upper mantle that may have been initiated by a meteorite, or that could just be an anomaly in the earth's crust. Over millions of years, this 'hot spot' has created the broad Snake River Plain, and it has caused major eruptions, producing large craters and calderas such as the Island Park caldera in Idaho and the Yellowstone caldera in Wyoming. Today, the hot spot is under Yellowstone NP, as indicated by the many geysers and hot springs there.

In some parts of the Northern US Rockies, spectacular mountains have been produced by massive fault blocks, but over millions of years many mountains in these dry climates have eroded to the point where they are almost buried by their own debris. Alternating wet eras have produced huge rivers that washed away debris and opened valleys. Continental glaciers have smoothed the plains and some peaks, and alpine glaciers have cut broad, U-shaped valleys and dramatic peaks in other areas. Some of the highest peaks in this region are Gannett Peak (4,208 m), Cloud Peak (4,001 m) and Granite Peak (3,901 m).

The **Southern US Rockies** extend from the Laramie Mountains and Sierra Madre Range in southern Wyoming to the Sangre de Cristo Range in New Mexico, bounded by the Great Plains on the east and by the Wyoming Basin and Colorado Plateau on the west. This region contains some of the highest mountains in the Rockies, with 54 summits over 4,270 m and over 1,000 peaks above 3,050 m. The highest mountains include Long's Peak (4,345 m), Gray's Peak (4,350 m), Mt. Evans (with seasonal road access to the summit at 4,348 m) and Mt. Elbert (4,399 m).

The Southern US Rockies can be divided into 2 major sections: the Eastern Ranges and the Western Ranges. The Eastern Ranges are composed mainly of sedimentary rock over crystalline rock cores. Many peaks have been sculpted by glaciers, and others show the effects of erosion by wind and water. The result is a variety of mountain types, including glaciated, snow-capped mountains with quartzitic peaks, unglaciated mountains buried in 100s of metres of debris and rounded granite knobs. Many volcanic mountains of lava and ash, with hot springs and geothermal reservoirs, are also in this region, and some ash deposits have been carved by wind and water to form spectacular canyons and mesas.

The Rocky Mountains form the **Continental Divide**, the height of land that separates rivers flowing west to the Pacific Ocean from those flowing north and east to the Arctic and Atlantic oceans. Some of North America's **largest rivers** begin as small streams in the Rocky Mountains. Much of the water in westward-flowing rivers in the US is re-routed via ditches and tunnels to urban centres on the east slope, and this now poses a major threat to the Colorado River.

Climate

Climate is highly variable in the Rocky Mountains, because this extensive mountain chain covers a wide range of elevations and latitudes. Changes in either of these parameters can have a major effect on local climate. A rise of 100 m in elevation has been equated to travelling over 300 km north.

Temperatures are generally cool in the mountains, with annual averages ranging from about 2.5° C in the Canadian Rockies to about 10° C in the Southern US Rockies. These cool temperatures are, in large part, because of the cooling associated with higher elevations. The standard temperature change or 'lapse rate' with increasing elevation is about -0.5° C to -1.0° C for every 100 m of elevation. It can easily be 10–15° C cooler on a mountain peak than in a valley bottom. Subalpine areas may also be cooled by cold, dense air flowing down from ice or frozen ground at higher elevations. Above 2,750 m elevation, freezing temperatures can occur on any night of the year.

At high elevations, temperatures can fluctuate greatly—heat is gained rapidly and then lost by radiation through the thinner atmosphere. Plants and animals at high elevations are also exposed to greater amounts of ultraviolet radiation, because the thinner atmosphere absorbs less incoming radiation. On a cloudless summer day, ultraviolet radiation is approximately 25 percent higher at 4,270 m than it is at 1,675 m. Also, at higher elevations, there is less oxygen. Many people experience shortness of breath above 2,440 m; air above 3,050 m has about two-thirds as much oxygen as air at sea level. Some visitors experience 'mountain sickness' or 'elevation sickness' in high areas, with headaches, nausea and general fatigue. It is recommended they allow themselves 2–3 days to acclimate before undertaking strenuous physical activity at high elevations.

Figure 1: Rocky Mountain Vegetation Zones

General Changes in Elevation With Latitude

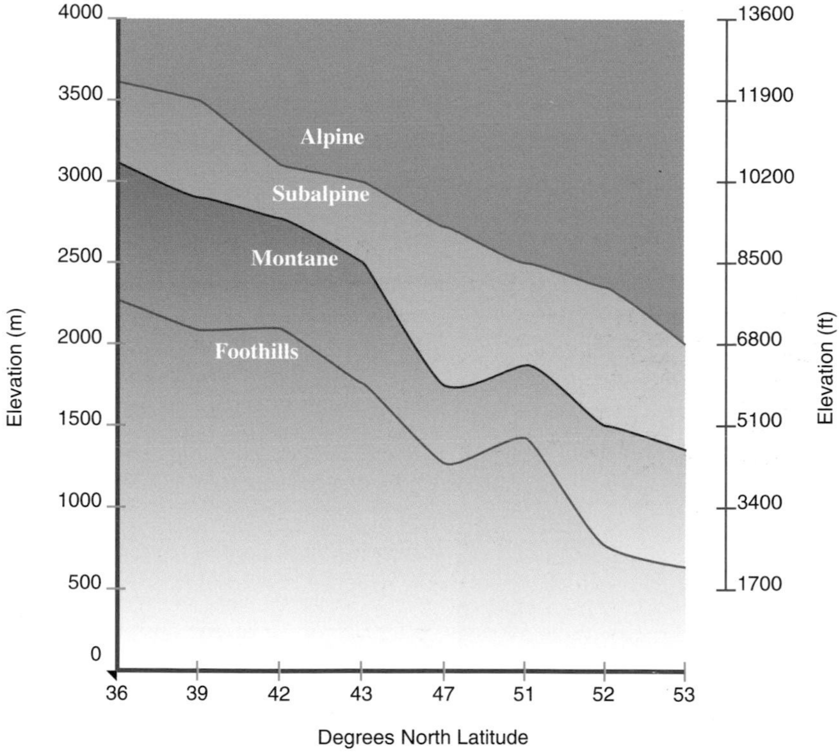

The mountain climate varies dramatically with changes in latitude, as temperatures decline from south to north. The effects of this change can be seen in the gradual lowering of the treeline (the edge of alpine tundra) from south to north. For example, treeline is generally at 3,300–3,600 m elevation in Colorado, whereas in Alberta it ranges from 2,000–2,300 m. As a general rule, treeline is said to shift by approximately 110 m with every degree of latitude.

Differences in temperature have a wide range of effects on these mountain landscapes. Southern areas are warmer, and with higher temperatures come increased evaporation, drier soils, smaller rivers, fewer glaciers and longer growing seasons. Southern parts of the Rockies are also drier because of their location farther inland from the Pacific. Prevailing winds blow from west to east across the Rockies, and as the air from the Pacific rises, it cools and drops much of its moisture as rain or snow on the western slopes, leaving the eastern slopes noticeably drier and cooler. The Canadian Rockies lie relatively closer to the Pacific coast, and they receive large amounts of rain- and snowfall as moisture-laden air rises to flow over their peaks. The Southern US Rockies, on the other hand, lie much farther inland, and air masses pass over a vast expanse of dry land called the Great Basin before they reach the eastern ranges of the cordillera, so prevailing winds in the south are much drier than those to the north.

About 75 percent of this precipitation falls west of the Continental Divide. The inland location of the Rockies, away from the moderating effects of the ocean, also results in greater daily and seasonal temperature fluctuations. There can also be huge year-to-year and decade-to-decade variations. Severe rainstorms and thunderstorms are common, and they frequently cause fires. Because of the influence of the Gulf of Mexico, Colorado has a 'monsoonal' climate, with thunderstorms almost every day in summer. The high summer moisture of the 'banana belt' around Denver results in vegetation with a much greater variety of plant species.

Vegetation

Environments change dramatically in the Rockies with changes in elevation and latitude, and these variations are reflected in a wide array of vegetation types (see Figure 1, p. 13). Although the plant communities are generally discussed by elevational zone, there are rarely clear lines dividing natural systems. Most plants grow in more than 1 type of plant community, and species from adjacent vegetation types often intermix, making these 'interfaces' some of the most diverse and productive biological zones.

Foothills Zone

The foothills in the **Canadian Rockies** are generally less clearly defined than those in the US, because in Canada, mountain forests slowly grade to boreal forest in the east and to the Columbian Forest in the west, both of which have many environmental characteristics and plant species in common with the ones of the Rockies. Foothills **forests** in the Canadian Rockies consist mainly of **lodgepole pine (*Pinus contorta*) and/or trembling aspen (*Populus tremuloides*)**, with shrub-dominated understoreys that include Canada buffaloberry (*Shepherdia canadensis*), prickly rose (*Rosa acicularis*), wild red raspberry (*Rubus idaeus*) and common bearberry (*Arctostaphylos uva-ursi*). In the southern part of the Canadian Rockies (i.e., south of Calgary), conditions are warmer and drier, grading to prairie (rather than boreal forest) in the east and to a broad, intermontane plain in the west. Here, the tree cover of foothills is less continuous, with stands of lodgepole pine interspersed with grassy slopes. Prickly-pear cactus (*Opuntia* spp.) and **ponderosa pine (*Pinus ponderosa*)** also grow on some of these dry, interior slopes.

In the **US Rockies**, the foothills are generally low elevation **scrublands** that form the transition between the prairie and the treed (montane) slopes. Shrubs first appear on cooler, moister, north-facing slopes and in valleys, but with increasing elevation, they gradually spread to south-facing slopes (as trees begin to appear in valleys and on north-facing slopes), and eventually they are replaced by the montane forests. Grasses provide scattered ground cover in these dry communities, with blue grama (*Bouteloua gracilis*), wheatgrasses (*Agropyron* spp.),

Junegrass (*Koeleria macrantha*), needle-and-thread grass (*Stipa comata*) and fescues (*Festuca* spp.). Such sites are easily damaged by fire, overgrazing and trampling, and disturbed areas are rapidly invaded by weeds. In wet years these shrublands are adorned with a surprising variety of wildflowers, including arrow-leaved balsamroot (*Balsamorhiza saggitata*), northern mule-ears (*Wyethia amplexicaulis*), larkspurs (*Delphinium* spp.), penstemons (*Penstemon* spp.), scarlet gilia (*Ipomopsis aggregata*) and fleabanes (*Erigeron* spp.).

The wide range of shrub communities in the **Northern US Rockies foothills** range from semi-desert species in the southwest to species with higher moisture requirements in the northwest. The most common shrubs are **junipers (*Juniperus* spp.), sagebrush (*Artemisia* spp.) and mahogany (*Cercocarpus* spp.)**. In intermontane valleys, big sagebrush (*Artemisia tridentata*) is very common, with thickets of taller shrubs such as chokecherry (*Prunus virginiana*), saskatoon (*Amelanchier alnifolia*) on higher slopes, merging with montane forests. Moist slopes can be covered with wasatch maple (*Acer grandidentatum*) and dry slopes are often blanketed with scrub oak (*Quercus* spp.) in both the Northern US and Southern US Rockies.

Much of the foothills of the **Southern US Rockies** is covered by dry, open **piñon-juniper woodlands**—sometimes called 'pygmy forests'—easily recognized by their low (usually less than 6 m tall), round-crowned trees of two-needle piñon (*Pinus edulis*) and/or junipers (*Juniperus* spp.). At higher elevations, scrub oak and other shrubs merge with montane forests and in the south, Apache plume (*Fallugia paradoxa*) is typical of the transition to ponderosa pine stands. **Sagebrush shrublands** are also widespread, dominated by dryland shrubs such as big sagebrush, common rabbitbush (*Chrysothamnus nauseosus*) and antelopebrush (*Purshia tridentata*). On higher slopes, **mountain shrublands** consist primarily of Gambel's oak (*Quercus gambelii*) on west- and south-facing slopes and mountain mahogany (*Cercocarpus montanus*) on north- and east-facing slopes. These shrubs often grow intermixed with skunkbush (*Rhus trilobata*), choke cherry and antelopebrush.

The sparse ground cover of Southern US Rockies foothills is dominated by grasses such as blue grama and Indian ricegrass (*Oryzopsis hymenoides*), but wildflowers such as prickly-pear cactus, gumweeds (*Grindelia* spp.), golden-aster (*Heterotheca villosa*) and fleabanes can also be common.

Montane Zone

The montane zone supports the greatest variety of wildflowers, trees and shrubs. It generally ranges from open stands at low elevations to dense forest as it merges with the subalpine. In the US Rockies, the montane zone is generally defined as the 'forested' zone immediately above the scrublands of the foothills, but in Canada it is less clearly defined. **Douglas-fir (*Pseudotsuga menziesii*)** is sometimes labelled as the species defining the extent of the montane zone, but it rarely common north of Calgary.

In the southern **Canadian Rockies**, Douglas-fir is widespread in the montane zone, and the transition from plains to montane follows a pattern similar to that of the US Rockies, with species from drier, prairie regions (e.g., moss phlox [*Phlox hoodii*], prairie sagewort [*Artemisia frigida*], Junegrass, creeping juniper and prairie crocus [Pulsatilla patens]) gradually replaced by mountain species in forests and rich meadows. Shrubs in this region include saskatoon, rose, snowberry (*Symphoricarpos* spp.) and choke cherry.

The montane zone in the rest of the Canadian Rockies is typically a cool, damp, continuous forest composed of a mix of widespread, northern species.

Lodgepole pine forests are the most common forest type in the Canadian montane zone. Lodgepole pine is a 'fire tree,' depending on forest fires to reproduce in large numbers and to avoid invasion by other, more shade-tolerant trees. Lodgepole pine stands are extremely dense and homogeneous when young, but as they mature they become more open, with a variety of shrubs in the understorey, including Canada buffaloberry, common bearberry, birch-leaved spirea (*Spiraea betulifolia*) and Utah honeysuckle (*Lonicera utahensis*). Common wildflowers in these forests include heart-leaved arnica (*Arnica cordifolia*), pussytoes (*Antennaria* spp.) and wintergreen (*Pyrola* spp.)

Trembling aspen forests are also common, mainly at low elevations. These open stands have relatively sunny understoreys, with a variety of wildflowers, including geranium (*Geranium* spp.), creamy peavine (*Lathyrus ochroleucus*), veiny meadowrue (*Thalictrum venulosum*), star-flowered Solomon's seal (*Maianthemum stellatum*) and Canada violet (*Viola canadensis*).

Along rivers and streams, **balsam poplar (*Populus balsamifera*)** is the most common tree. All 3 of these forest types need repeated disturbance if they are to persist for long periods of time. Left undisturbed, they may eventually be replaced by dense, shaded stands of Engelmann spruce (*Picea engelmannii*), white spruce (*Picea glauca*) and/or subalpine fir (*Abies bifolia*).

In the US Rockies, **young montane and subalpine forests** are usually composed of lodgepole pine (drier sites) and trembling aspen (moister sites), similar to those found in the Canadian Rockies. Both trees have broad latitudinal (i.e., Alaska to Mexico) and elevational (i.e., 1,500–3,500 m) ranges, both are aggressive invaders of disturbed sites, and both are maintained by disturbances such as fire, logging or erosion.

Trembling aspen forests grow in a wide range of sites, and stand characteristics vary from tall trees above lush, tangled understorey shrubs (e.g., red osier dogwood [*Cornus sericea*]) to dry, exposed slopes with stunted trees above scattered shrubs (e.g., Rocky Mountain ninebark [*Physocarpus monogynus*]). Aspen also grows intermixed with other trees in many regions.

Lodgepole pine forests are commonly established following forest fires, but they can also develop when forests are removed by extensive insect infestations or logging. The dense, extensive monocultures of younger stands are monotonous and somewhat biologically impoverished, because they exclude most other plants, and provide limited habitat for most animals. Older stands gradually become more open and support understorey shrubs such as common juniper (*Juniperus communis*), prairie rose (*Rosa woodsii*) and common bearberry. Some parasitic and saprophytic plants that do not require sunlight survive in these shady sites. They include coralroots (*Corallorhiza* spp.), pinedrops (*Pterospora andromedea*) and dwarf mistletoes (*Arceuthobium* spp.).

Douglas-fir forests are characteristic of much of the **montane zone of the Northern US Rockies**. Similar stands are also present in the Southern US Rockies at high elevations and on cool, moist sites at low elevations. Beards (*Usnea* spp.) are common on shaded lower branches of mature stands, and white fir (*Abies concolor*) is often a co-dominant tree. Douglas-fir often grows inter-mixed with many different trees, and the understorey is generally sparse, with low shrubs such as falsebox (*Paxistima myrsinites*), common bearberry and common juniper. Moist sites are carpeted with a thick mat of mosses and lichens, and wildflowers include Venus'-slipper (*Calypso bulbosa*), twinflower (*Linnaea borealis*) and heart-leaved arnica.

Ponderosa pine forests are characteristic of the montane zone in the Southern US Rockies. They also grow in the lower montane and upper foothills in the Northern US Rockies. These stately, open stands need recurrent, low-intensity fires to maintain their park-like appearance. The understorey is typically sparse, with shrubs such as squaw currant (*Ribes cereum*), mountain mahogany, common bearberry, common juniper, big sagebrush, and antelope brush, and luxuriant growth of grasses such as mountain muhly (*Muhlenbergia montana*) and timber oatgrass (*Danthonia intermedia*). Wildflowers include prairie crocus, hedgehog cactus (*Pediocactus simpsonii*) and sulphur buckwheat (*Eriogonum umbellatum*). These dry, open stands interfinger with Douglas-fir and spruce forests in cooler, moister areas at higher elevations and on north-facing slopes

Limber pine (*Pinus flexilis*) stands are widespread on exposed ridges, and beautiful meadows and open, park-like stands are common along mountain streams in broad valleys in the US Rockies.

Subalpine Zone

The subalpine zone extends from the upper edge of the montane forest to the lower edge of the treeless, alpine zone. It is sometimes said to end at 'timberline' (the upper limit of fully erect trees), but for the purposes of this guide the upper limit is set at 'treeline' (the upper limit of all trees), so the subalpine zone includes stands of stunted, twisted trees (krummholz stands) that extend into alpine meadows at high elevations. Subalpine forests are sometimes called 'snow forests' because they grow at elevations where moisture (both rain and snow) is high, and their dense trees protect the thick snowpack from melting and evaporating in spring. Many delicate, moisture-loving wildflowers grow in this zone.

The subalpine zone is fairly uniform throughout the Rocky Mountains. It consists primarily of dense, almost continuous forests of **subalpine fir and/or Engelmann spruce** with mossy forest floors supporting low shrubs such as grouseberry (*Vaccinium scoparium*), black elderberry (*Sambucus racemosa*), squashberry (*Viburnum edule*) and Canada buffaloberry. Crowberry (*Empetrum nigrum*) and Labrador tea (*Ledum groenlandicum*) are also common in the Canadian Rockies, and falsebox is common in the US Rockies.

Small, pale wildflowers such as prince's pine (*Chimaphila umbellata*) and one-flowered wintergreen (*Moneses uniflora*) live in the shelter of these dense forests, but a vast array of beautiful mountain wildflowers grows in the moist, sheltered meadows between scattered stands of trees in the upper subalpine. Some of the most common are yellow columbine (*Aquilegia flavescens*), cut-leaved anemone (*Anemone multifida*), yellow glacier-lily (*Erythronium grandiflorum*), cow parsnip (*Heracleum lanatum*), tall Jacob's ladder (*Polemonium acutiflorum*), arrow-leaved groundsel (*Senecio triangularis*) and subalpine fleabane (*Erigeron peregrinus*).

Short (usually less than 30 ft tall), gnarled **limber pine and whitebark pine (*Pinus albicaulis*)** trees often grow scattered on dry, exposed slopes or in open stands in the foothills, montane and subalpine zones from Banff south to New

Mexico. Large taproots anchor these trees to their rocky slopes, and flexible branches bend rather than break in the mountain winds. These long-lived trees (sometimes more than 1,000 years old) persevere under extreme conditions. The sparse understorey includes shrubs like common juniper, shrubby cinquefoil (*Pentaphylloides floribunda*), common bearberry and snowbrush (*Ceanothus velutinus*) as well as herbs like spotted saxifrage (*Saxifraga bronchialis*), Labrador tea, common alumroot (*Heuchera parvifolia*) and silky scorpionweed (*Phacelia sericea*).

Alpine (*Tundra*) Zone

The alpine zone extends from treeline to the end of vegetation on exposed, rocky slopes or at the edge of permanent snowfields at high elevations. In this cold, windswept environment, some areas may be free of snow early in spring (and even through most of winter) and others lie blanketed with drifts for most or all of summer. The alpine flower display on mountain tops usually peaks in July—a date influenced more by snow accumulation than by latitude. Snow provides warmer, more constant soil and air temperatures, higher humidity and soil moisture, and protection from drying and abrasion by wind, but too much can reduce the already short growing season.

The alpine tundra is a fine-grained mosaic of vegetation, where plants survive near their limits, and minor changes in moisture, exposure and substrate can mean the difference between life and death. A rise a few centimetres high can change radiation levels, wind strength and snow accumulation levels to the point where a small plant can begin to grow.

Alpine plants tend to be small, low-growing and adapted to rapid growth in the short, cold summers. Almost all are perennial. Many are found throughout the Rockies, and at least 20 percent have ranges that extend around the world in the Arctic.

Alpine plant communities are similar throughout the Rocky Mountains. Moist **alpine meadows** support lush mats of sedges and herbs, including arrow-leaved grounsel, sitka valerian (*Valeriana sitchensis*), arctic lupine (*Lupinus arcticus*), scarlet paintbrush (*Castilleja miniata*), anemones (*Anemone* spp.) and alpine bluebells (*Mertensia alpina*). In drier, more exposed areas, herbs are more scattered, and include low wildflowers such as arctic harebell (*Campanula uniflora*), moss gentian (*Gentiana prostrata*), forget-me-nots (*Eritrichium* spp.) and western yellow paintbrush (*Castilleja occidentalis*). Inconspicuous sedges such as bog sedge (*Kobresia myosuroides*), kobresia-like sedge (*Carex elynoides*) and curly sedge (*Carex rupestris*) cover much of these slopes, and the 'climax' vegetation may be a tight, short, sedge turf that excludes most other plants.

In drier **rock fields**, plants grow scattered among rocks in moist cracks and crevices. Many form dense cushions (e.g., moss campion [*Silene acaulis*], cushion phlox [*Phlox pulvinata*], one-flowered cinquefoil [*Potentilla uniflora*], alpine sandwort [*Minuartia obtusiloba*], pale alpine forget-me-not [*Eritrichium nanum*]) or mats (e.g. white mountain avens [*Dryas octopetala*], dwarf clover [*Trifolium nanum*] and dwarf willows [*Salix* spp.]). These growth forms reduce water loss and retain warmth. The less densely matted plants in these communities include alpine anemone (*Anemone drummondii*), alpine pussytoes (*Antennaria alpina*), alpine milk-vetch (*Astragalus alpinus*), cut-leaved fleabane (*Erigeron compositus*), sweet-vetch (*Hedysarum* spp.), cinquefoil (*Potentilla* spp.), saxifrage (*Saxifraga* spp.), roseroot (*Sedum integrifolium*), alpine avens (*Geum rossii*) and draba (*Draba* spp.).

Some alpine plants have adapted for survival on steeper, less stable, rocky slopes (**scree and talus slopes**). They include alpine smelowskia (*Smelowskia calycina*), sticky Jacob's ladder (*Polemonium viscosum*), dwarf hawksbeard (*Crepis nana*) and mountain sorrel (*Oxyria digyna*).

Late snow patches provide abundant moisture, but short growing seasons. Plants that grow in these habitats often reproduce vegetatively (by sending out new shoots) because they don't have time to flower and produce seed. In the Canadian Rockies, areas with late-lying snow often support mats of low evergreen shrubs (heaths), including mountain-heather (*Cassiope* spp.), crowberry and partridgefoot (*Luetkea pectinata*). However, common species through most of the Rockies include spiked sedge (*Carex pyrenaica*), alpine pussytoes, Drummond's rush (*Juncus drummondii*), sibbaldia (*Sibbaldia procumbens*), white buttercup (*Ranunculus nivalis*), alpine willowherb (*Epilobium anagallidifolium*) and Ross' avens (*Geum rossii*).

Disturbed Habitats

Many of the most common wildflowers along roads and in fields and towns did not grow here less than 200 years ago. These highly successful plants, or 'weeds,' were introduced to North America by humans. Most originated in Europe and Asia. Some arrived accidentally, mixed with other plant products such as seed or hay, but many were brought here purposely as crops, medicinal plants and garden flowers. Since their arrival, many of the hardier and more aggressive plants have spread across the continent. Most seem to prefer disturbed ground, often associated with human activity, but others are expanding into natural habitats, where they can replace less-aggressive native plants. The most successful invaders are classified as 'noxious weeds,' and although many are very pretty, they are troublesome pests in the human setting, and a threat to plant communities in the wild.

Common weeds include spotted knapweed (*Centaurea maculosa*), chicory (*Cichorium intybus*), oxeye daisy (*Leucanthemum vulgare*), pineapple weed (*Matricaria matricarioides*), perennial sow-thistle (*Sonchus arvensis*), common tansy (*Tanacetum vulgare*), common dandelion (*Taraxacum officinale*), yellow salsify (*Tragpogon dubius*), teasel (*Dipsacus sylvestris*), alfalfa (*Medicago sativa*), meadow buttercup (*Ranunculus acris*), great mullein (*Verbascum thapsus*), annual hawksbeard (*Crepis tectorum*), Canada thistle (*Cirsium arvense*), bull thistle (*Cirsium vulgare*), common toadflax (*Linaria vulgaris*), yellow sweet-clover (*Melilotus officinalis*), red clover (*Trifolium pratense*), white clover (*T. repens*) and alsike clover (*T. hybridum*).

The Role of Fire

Fire is one of the most important natural factors controlling ecosystems and landscapes in the Rocky Mountains. Deciduous trees and many pines and larches need fire to reproduce by seed. In drier forests, fires also maintain open stands that support a wide array of plants and are more able to resist insects and disease.

Three main types of fire behaviour occur in the Rockies. In dense high-elevation forests where slowly melting snow provides adequate moisture for most of the year, stands only dry sufficiently to burn during periods of drought. Droughts usually affect broad regions, so these fires tends to be large and catastrophic. An example is the huge Yellowstone fire in 1988. The second major fire type has small ground fires in dry forests near the lower montane zone. Ponderosa pine forests are usually affected by this type of fire. These fires can recur as often as every 1–2 years in the Southern US Rockies, and as infrequently as every 5–25 years in the Northern US Rockies, but they kill few trees, while maintaining an open forest. The third type—'mixed replacement' fire—often affects many Douglas-fir or lodgepole pine forests on dry sites. Such fires change in intensity as they move across the mountain, fluctuating between intense burns that kill large trees and low-intensity ground fires that kill only small trees and shrubs. All 3 fire types have influenced the complex mosaic of forests in the Rockies today, and fire remains a key factor in maintaining the natural diversity of this region.

Since the 1930s, fire control programs have greatly reduced small ground fires and mixed-replacement fires in the Rockies, and as a result much denser forests have developed, and forests have encroached upon some grasslands and meadows. Species associated with younger, more open ecosystems (e.g., larch, trembling aspen, ponderosa pine) are declining, and when the dense, fuel-rich forests do burn, they typically produce large-scale, catastrophic fires. Efforts to reintroduce fire into natural systems are controversial. Natural fires are being allowed to burn in some areas to help reduce the chances of a catastrophic fire later. Low-intensity burns are soon blanketed with wildflowers and shrubs, because they have warmer, richer and less acidic soil.

Wildlife

The large tracts of wilderness in the Rocky Mountains, with their diverse habitats, provide homes for many animals. Moose, elk and deer live in most regions, and bison have been re-introduced to some parts of the US Rockies and to the northern Canadian Rockies. Goats and bighorn sheep live in subalpine and alpine regions. Black bears (and in the Canadian Rockies, grizzly bears, wolves and pumas) still roam many slopes, providing wildlife viewing opportunities and occasional safety concerns. Small mammals, including hares, minks, squirrels and chipmunks, abound in the forests; muskrats and beavers are widespread in wetlands; and marmots and pikas can be found at higher elevations. Bird life is also abundant and diverse, ranging from majestic eagles soaring on updrafts, to a variety of 'camp-robbers' (usually members of the overly intelligent crow family) and small, secretive songbirds in the forest. Fish are plentiful in the clear mountain rivers, streams and lakes.

PLANTS AND PEOPLE

Very few native peoples lived in the Rocky Mountains year-round. Most spent the cold, snowy winter months at lower elevations nearby and travelled to the mountains during summer to hunt or gather plants. Native peoples in the Rocky Mountain region are generally classified as belonging to the Plateau Region (from just south of Jasper to about central Idaho) or the Great Basin Region (from central Idaho to northern New Mexico). North of this region, they are considered to be in the Western Sub-arctic Region (see general distributions, Map p. 21).

Hunting and fishing were the mainstays of life for **Western Sub-Arctic** peoples. Animals, especially large ungulates, provided most of their food, clothing and shelter. Most fish and game were taken during the summer and fall, and the meat was dried in thin strips and stored in caches for later use. Some berries, bulbs and shoots were eaten in season, but animal derived food often comprised over 90 percent of their diet.

Winters in the Canadian Rockies are long and cold, so winter clothing included fur coats and leggings, moccasins and snowshoes. Winter homes were made of wooden frames covered with moose or caribou hides and/or spruce bows and bark, and then banked with snow for further insulation. In summer, people moved around in small, extended family groups or bands. Tribal borders shifted with time, and bands were not always clearly delineated, because membership frequently shifted between groups.

For tribes in the **Plateau Region**, food gathering tended to be more important than hunting. There was also a considerable dependence on salmon, which were usually gathered at fishing

NATIVE AMERICAN AREAS
(after Spencer et al. 1977)

camps. These needs led to a more sedentary life, and with this came a sense of tribe, which developed further under the influence of Plains tribes. People identified with local groups (e.g., autonomous villages), but the lines between political units were often hazy. Most people lived in small villages of 150–200 people. Each settlement had hunting grounds, fishing stations and gathering places.

Mats were widely used in the construction of communal winter homes or smaller, single-family summer homes. The large winter homes could be either above-ground structures or excavated earth lodges. Mats had many other uses, including bedding, drying food and wrapping corpses. A good deal of time and skill went into weaving mats, which was done by the women, and therefore the mats were usually taken along when the family moved. However, if a death had occurred in a house, the structure was burned, because it was believed that illness would otherwise dog the inhabitants in the future.

Only the women gathered roots and fruits. Small groups of families travelled to the plains to gather roots, leaving the aged and infirm in the winter village. Women worked together under the leadership of an older woman who decided where, when and what would be collected. Roots, tubers and stem plants were gathered through summer, and many were dried and carried back to the winter camp for storage. In some areas, large quantities of 'wokas' (the seeds of water lilies and pond lilies) were collected. In autumn, women might travel short distances to collect different kinds of berries, many of which were pounded together with fat and venison to make pemmican.

Only men were allowed to fish, and women were often barred from places where fish might be disturbed. The fishing season lasted from early May to October. A variety of fish, including fresh-water whitefish, suckers and even sturgeon were taken, but salmon was the staple food of many tribes on tributaries of the Fraser and Columbia rivers. Fish were caught with spears and traps, usually at sites where rapids forced rivers into narrow channels. Sometimes, short, artificial channels were dug and lined with white stones, and platforms were built so that spearers could stand above the water. A Salmon Chief (a shaman or a man with the salmon as one of his guardian spirits) often directed the timing and manning of fishing activities, the distribution of the catch, and religious ceremonies associated with fishing. If a shaman from another village caused the salmon run to stop, the local shaman had to use his power to restore the run, and perhaps to send illness and death in return. Although women were not allowed to catch fish, they cleaned the catch, dried the fish on racks for about 10–14 days, and stored it in sewn bags. In cool weather, salmon was dried indoors and inadvertently smoked. In autumn, when the women gathered berries, the men moved to the wooded mountains to hunt for large animals such as deer, elk and bears. Small groups were led by a skilled hunter who had one of the animals as his guardian spirit. Wolves, foxes and other fur bearers were taken in traps and deadfalls. Rabbits were often shot with arrows. They were especially important for making clothing, such as mittens and caps, and blankets.

During winter, people generally remained indoors in communal dwellings. This was a time for dancing, gambling and story-telling.

The **Great Basin** was inhabited by wandering people who spent much of their time travelling in search of wild seeds. Two-needle piñon was often a staple food. Game was never plentiful in the dry regions at low elevations, though there were occasional rabbit hunts and communal antelope drives. Some hunters travelled to the coniferous forests in the higher mountains in search of deer, but gathering was much more important than hunting.

Over 100 plant species were collected by the Great Basin people. Both men and women took part in the work. Many plants were woven, coiled and twined by women into a variety of baskets, including burden baskets, basketry seed beaters, winnowing baskets, parching trays, water baskets (tightly coiled and covered with pitch) and cooking baskets (with a rack in the bottom for hot stones used to bring water to a boil). A variety of seeds were used for food. Some were eaten raw and others were parched; some were coarsely ground and used to make mush or gruel, while others were ground into flour and baked as cakes. Roots were collected using a digging stick. Most were boiled in pots or baskets, or roasted in ashes. In autumn, after the first frosts at high altitudes had split the cones, groups of families gathered pine cones (knocking them from trees with hooked sticks) and collected the pine nuts.

Virtually all large animals were hunted or trapped (e.g., sheep, deer, rodents, snakes, lizards, birds and fish), but the coyote was thought to have human qualities, so it was not killed. Insects, including grasshoppers, locusts, ants, bees, caterpillars and insect larvae and eggs, were often used for food. Mormon crickets were avidly sought when they appeared in vast numbers every 7 years. Rabbits were hunted communally using nets made by men from strings of hemp dogbane (*Apocynum cannabinum*) fibres. Some rabbit nets were over 1.5 km (1 mile) long, and they were so important that they might be inherited, and the owner would then be recognized as chief of the hunt. Rabbits were used for their meat, and their skins were cut into long strings and woven together with a variety of other fibres to make rabbit-skin blankets.

As in the Plateau Region, woven mats were used to make shelters. These ranged from temporary windbreaks in summer to large, cone-shaped lodges in winter. Winter lodges were often subterranean, and they could also be covered with bark, brush, grass or earth. In some tribes, men and women were tattooed on the face, arms and legs, using a cactus needle to make designs with charcoal and burned two-needle piñon shells.

East of the Rockies, tribes from the **Plains Region** often travelled into the mountains to hunt and gather plants. These people were nomadic bison hunters, relying on the meat and hides of bison and other large animals for food, clothing and shelter. Belongings had to be light, compact and durable, because they were frequently packed up and loaded onto travois as the band followed the bison or moved to new areas in search of roots and berries. Many traits of the Plains Indians, including the use of horses, tipis and patterned warfare, were adopted by tribes to the west.

Ethnobotany

Ethnobotany is the study of the relationships between people and plants. The importance of plants varied greatly throughout the Rockies. Trees provided wood, pitch, bark and roots, mosses provided absorbent diapers, and a wide range of plants provided medicines and food. The ethnobotanical information in this book was taken from many sources (see the 'References' section). Whenever possible, the uses of plants by people in the Rocky Mountains was reported, but information is sometimes presented about the history of use in other areas such as eastern North America and Europe.

PLEASE NOTE: This book records many historical uses of plants. Such information is presented to give the reader a better sense of the rich cultural and natural heritage of this region. **This guide is not meant to be a 'how-to' reference for consuming wild plants. We do not recommend experimentation by readers and we caution that many of the plants in the Rocky Mountains, including some traditional medicines, are poisonous and harmful.**

TREES

Trees are single-stemmed, woody plants that are greater than 10 m in height when mature. Some small trees (e.g., alder, Rocky Mountain juniper, western yew) rarely reach 10 m in height, and these are included in the Shrubs section (pp. 41–81). Although several willow species (notably Scouler's and Bebb's willows) can grow to greater than 10 m in height, they are included with the other willows (pp. 49–54) in the Shrubs section.

Key to Tree Genera

1a. Leaves needle-like or scale-like, mostly evergreen; seeds in cones, not enclosed in a fruit (conifers) 2

2a. Leaves mostly scale-like and pressed against the twig, less than 5 mm long; bark often shredding and forming narrow, flat ridges on old trunks .... ***Thuja*** (p. 32)

2b. Leaves needle-like and spreading from twigs, usually more than 1 cm long 3

3a. Leaves (needles) in clusters of 2 or more 4

4a. Needles deciduous, in clusters of 15–30, on woody, barrel-shaped projections from twigs .... ***Larix*** (p. 33)

4b. Needles in clusters of 2, 3 or 5 .... ***Pinus*** (p. 34)

3b. Leaves (needles) borne singly on twig, not in clusters 5

5a. Needles 4-sided, 4-angled in cross-section, mostly 1–3 cm long; mature bark thin and scaly .... ***Picea*** (p. 28)

5b. Needles flattened or semi-circular in cross-section, mostly 2–4.5 cm long; mature bark various 6

6a. Needles stalkless, curved upwards; young bark smooth, grey, with resin blisters; buds greater than 0.5 cm long, blunt-tipped; crown spire-like .... ***Abies*** (p. 27)

6b. Needles stalked, not curved upwards; young bark lacking resin blisters; buds 0.1–0.3 cm long or, if longer, then conical and sharp-pointed; crown various 7

7a. Cone bracts 3-pronged and prominent (usually longer than scales); buds conical and sharp-pointed; needles usually all the same length, flat, usually sharp-pointed; needle and stalk falling together leaving smooth, oval scars; crown not nodding at tip .... ***Pseudotsuga*** (p. 30)

7b. Cone bracts tiny, not 3-pronged; buds blunt-tipped; needles often of unequal lengths and rounded on top, rounded or indented at tips; needles falling from raised, woody bases with scars pointing forwards on twig; crown usually nodding at tip .... ***Tsuga*** (p. 31)

1b. Leaves broad and annually deciduous; seed enclosed in a fruit 8

8a. Bark with many conspicuous horizontal markings (lenticels) and peeling in large sheets; twigs dark reddish-brown; leaves single (alternate) on outer twigs, but appearing to be in pairs on inner branches .... ***Betula*** (p. 39)

8b. Bark lacking conspicuous horizontal markings and not peeling in sheets; twigs brownish-grey or orangy-grey; leaves single (alternate) on all twigs .... ***Populus*** (p. 37)

Abies bifolia (p. 27) *Picea engelmannii* (p. 28) *Picea glauca* (p. 29) *Pseudotsuga menziesii* (p. 30)

Tsuga heterophylla (p. 31) *Thuja plicata* (p. 32) *Larix occidentalis* (p. 33) *Pinus contorta* (p. 34) *Pinus ponderosa* (p. 36)

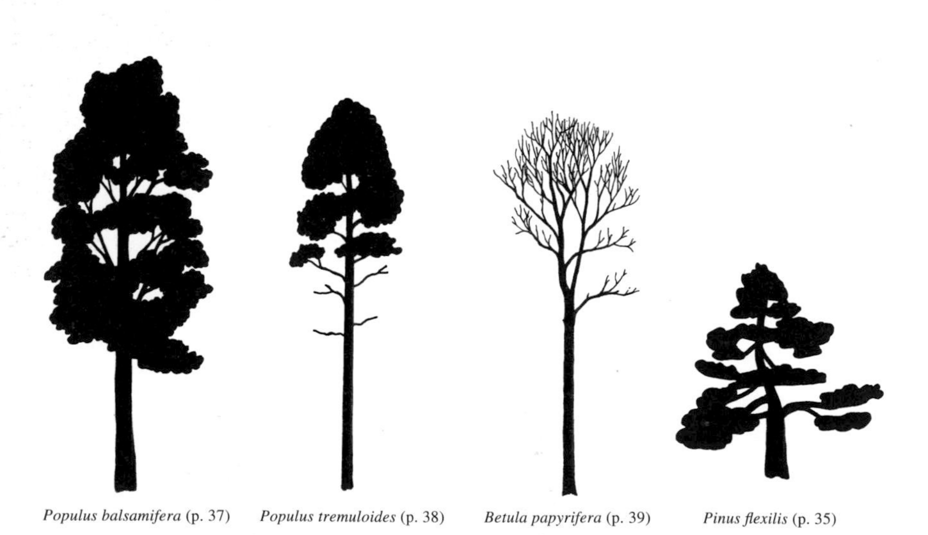

Populus balsamifera (p. 37) *Populus tremuloides* (p. 38) *Betula papyrifera* (p. 39) *Pinus flexilis* (p. 35)

SUBALPINE FIR
Abies bifolia

General: Coniferous tree, usually 20–35 m tall, often stunted and twisted (bonsai-like) near timberline, fragrant; branches short, thick; trunk 10–100 cm in diameter; **crown spire-like**.

Bark: Grey, thin, smooth, with **bulging resin blisters**.

Leaves: Evergreen **needles, 2–4 cm long**, usually blunt but some also pointed, flattened, **bluish-green** with rows of tiny, white dots (stomata) on both sides, crowded and tending to turn upwards.

Cones: Male and female cones on same tree; pollen (male) cones bluish, about 1 cm long, hanging; **seed (female) cones cylindrical**, 5–10 cm long, 3–3.5 cm thick, **sitting upright on upper branches, deep purple when young**, lighter with age, **shedding scales with seeds**, leaving only the slender central core; produced June to July, mature in 1 season.

Where Found: Mountain slopes; subalpine to alpine; the southern Yukon to New Mexico.

Notes: This species was once included in ***A. lasiocarpa***, but these 2 are now recognized as distinct. They have chemical differences, and the leaf scars of *A. bifolia* reveal a tan-coloured underlying layer (periderm), whereas in *A. lasiocarpa* this layer is red. Also, the triangular, basal bud scales of *A. lasiocarpa* have 3 equal, shallowly toothed sides, whereas those of *A. bifolia* are smooth-edged, with only 2 equal sides. The range of *A. lasiocarpa* extends from the Yukon and BC south through the coastal ranges to California. • **White fir** (***A. concolor***) has longer (4–7 cm), flatter needles that are generally twisted to spread in 2 opposite, flat rows. It grows on slopes in the montane zone from southern Idaho and Wyoming to New Mexico. • **Grand fir** (***A. grandis***) has 3–4 cm long, blunt to notched needles with lines of white stomata on the lower surface only. Like white fir, it has needles in 2 opposite, flat rows. It grows in foothills and montane zones from southeastern BC to Idaho and Wyoming. • Needles, pounded to powder and mixed with deer grease, were used as a pleasant-smelling hair tonic. Similar preparations provided salves to treat cuts, wounds, ulcers, sores, bleeding gums and skin infections. Finely ground needles were used to treat open, runny sores, and were also used as baby powder, body scent and as perfume or insect repellent for clothing. Bark gum was a handy antiseptic for wounds, cuts and bruises. Resin or needle tea was taken for colds. Needles were used in poultices to treat fevers and chest colds, or they were burned as incense. • Burning fir incense or hanging fir branches on walls was thought to chase away bad spirits and ghosts and to revive the spirits of people near death. • Under heavy snow and in krummholz stands at timberline, lower branches may become rooted, forming a circle of small trees around the parent tree. Squirrels harvest seeds from the cones in autumn. • The genus name *Abies* was derived from the Latin *abeo,* 'to rise' or 'arising,' because these trees spring so straight from the ground. The species name *lasiocarpa* is from the Greek *lasi,* 'hairy' or 'shaggy,' and *carpos,* 'fruit,' perhaps in reference to the slender tails on the bracts, which project out past the tips of the scales at pollination time, giving the cone a bristly appearance.

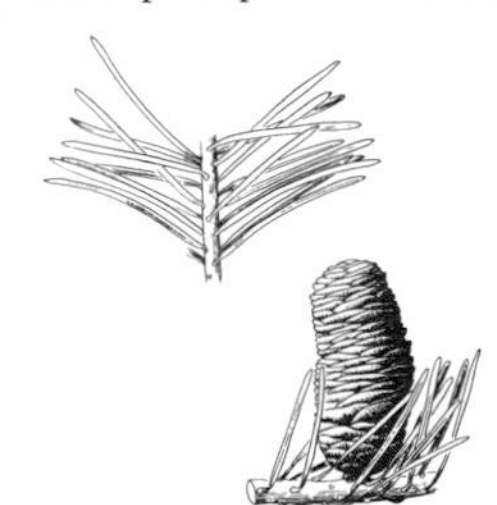

A. grandis *A. concolor*

ENGELMANN SPRUCE
Picea engelmannii

General: Coniferous, evergreen tree, usually 25–40 m tall, often stunted and shrub-like near timberline; trunk 30–90 cm in diameter; branches usually whorled; twigs with small stubs **left by old needles**, often minutely hairy; crown narrow, pyramid-like.

Bark: Light brown to grey, thin, forming loose scales; inner bark silvery-white.

Leaves: Evergreen **needles, blue-green, 4-sided, 2–3 cm long, sharp, somewhat flexible**, tending **to curve upwards and towards branch tips**, borne on persistent stubs, strong-smelling when crushed.

Cones: Male and female cones on same tree; pollen (male) cones dark purple to yellow, 10–15 mm long; seed (female) cones reddish to purplish when young, light chestnut-brown at maturity, oblong, usually 4–5 cm long, with **thin, flexible scales narrowed and jagged at tips**, hanging; produced June to July, open in autumn and fall intact in winter.

Where Found: Cool, moist slopes and ravines; montane to subalpine; BC and southwestern Alberta to New Mexico.

Notes: Colorado blue spruce (***P. pungens***) has darker, thicker, ridged bark, stiffer and sharper needles, hairless twigs and larger cones (usually 7–8 cm long) with rounded scales. One study showed that natural hybrids between Engelmann spruce and Colorado blue spruce do not occur. Colorado blue spruce grows along streams and in canyons from Wyoming to New Mexico. • Engelmann spruce can be confused with white spruce (p. 29), but the scales of white spruce cones are stiffer, with smooth, rounded tips. These 2 species often hybridize, and their offspring (*P. glauca* x *engelmannii)* are sometimes called 'interior spruce.' • Engelmann spruce is very cold tolerant. Mature trees can tolerate summer temperatures well below freezing and winter temperatures as low as -60° C. They are also very long lived, and can reach 1,000 years of age. • Northern tribes used Engelmann spruce bark to make canoes, and they used the split roots to sew baskets and canoes. The sticky sap (pitch) was used as a poultice for slivers and sores, branch tips were boiled to make a purifying wash, and emerging needles were chewed to relieve coughs. • The strong, uniform wood is used for lumber, plywood, mine timbers, poles and railway ties. Its long fibres, light colour and low resin content make it excellent pulp wood. Because of its resonance, it is also used to make piano-sounding boards and violins. • Deer and sheep browse the twigs, porcupines eat the inner bark, and chipmunks, squirrels, grouse and many other birds eat the seeds. • The genus name, *Picea*, was derived from the Latin *pix*, 'pitch.' The species name *engelmannii* commemorates George Engelmann (1809–84), a German botanist, physician and meteorologist who moved to St. Louis to travel and study plants (especially conifers) in the western US. His personal herbarium, which included the plant collections of many others, initiated the great Missouri Botanical Garden Herbarium.

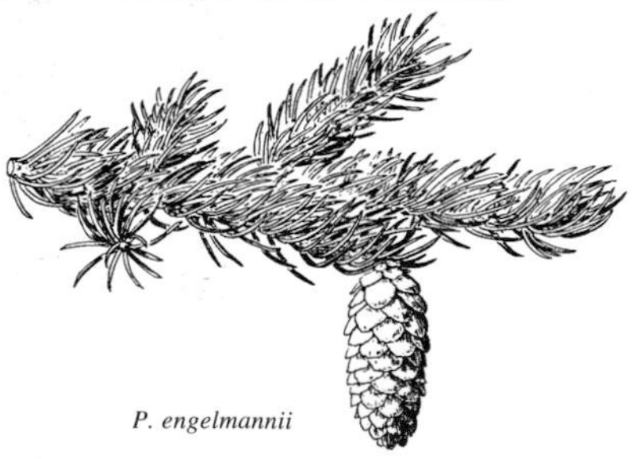
P. engelmannii

P. pungens

WHITE SPRUCE
Picea glauca

General: Coniferous, evergreen tree, usually 15–35 m tall; trunk 30–75 cm in diameter; twigs smooth, not hairy, with **stubs left by old needles**; branches numerous, often reaching the ground; crown narrowly to broadly pyramid-like.

Bark: Greyish-brown, forming loose, irregular scales; **inner bark tinged pink**.

Leaves: Evergreen **needles, bluish-green, 4-sided, 12–20 mm long (usually less than 15 mm), sharp-pointed**, stiff, straight, spreading from all sides of branches (**bottlebrush-like**), but sometimes more numerous on upper side, strong-smelling when crushed.

Cones: Male and female cones on same tree; pollen (male) cones pale red, 1–1.5 cm long; seed (female) cones purplish when young, light brown when mature, oblong, 2.5–4 cm long, **with thin, firm, rounded scales**, hanging; produced May to June, open in autumn, falling intact in winter.

Where Found: Well-drained, moist sites; foothills to subalpine; Alaska to northern Montana.

Notes: Black spruce (***P. mariana***) (bottom left photo) is a northern species that grows in the Rockies from central BC and Alberta to Alaska. It is distinguished by the tiny, rusty hairs on its young twigs and by its smaller cones (1–3 cm long) that persist for several years (rather than being shed each year). On dry sites, black spruce is difficult to distinguish from white spruce at a distance, but in cold, northern wetlands it has a distinctive, club-like silhouette with a dense, rounded crown above very short middle branches. • North of central Alberta, white spruce replaces Engelmann spruce (p. 28), but where their ranges overlap, these 2 species often hybridize. • Spruce beer was very important in preventing scurvy among early travellers in the north. The crew of the famous explorer, James Cook (1728–79), received a ration of spruce beer every day. • Native peoples mixed white spruce sap (pitch) with fat to make salves for treating skin infections, insect bites, chapped hands, cuts, scrapes, burns and rashes. The sap was also applied directly to skin problems, and the young growth was boiled to make an antiseptic wash. Dried sap (gum) was chewed, and boiled pitch was taken like cough syrup, to relieve coughs and sore throats. • Melted pitch was used to caulk canoe seams and to stick sheets of birch bark or strands of willow bark twine together. It was also used to preserve and waterproof strips of hide (babiche) in ropes, snares and snowshoes. Fresh or soaked white spruce roots were peeled and split to make cord for stitching canoes and baskets and for making fishnets. Split roots were also woven into water-tight bags for cooking. • Lumps of dried pitch were sometimes chewed like gum, which was said to kept the teeth white. • White spruce is the provincial tree of Manitoba.

DOUGLAS-FIR
Pseudotsuga menziesii

General: Coniferous, evergreen tree, 25–40 m tall; trunk straight, up to 1.5 m in diameter; branches irregular, spreading or drooping, tipped with **pointed, shiny, reddish-brown buds**; crown compact, pyramidal.

Bark: Grey-brown, **thin and smooth** with resin blisters **when young**, 8–20 cm thick with **corky ridges** and vertical fissures **when mature**.

Leaves: Flat, evergreen needles, spirally arranged, but often appearing to be **flattened in 2 rows**, 2–3 cm long, dark yellow to blue-green, **not sharp** to touch, aromatic when crushed; live 7–10 years.

Cones: Male and female cones on same tree; pollen (male) cones 6–8 mm long, reddish to yellow; seed (female) cones narrowly egg-shaped, 5–10 cm long, hanging, greenish when young, reddish-brown when mature; **scales stiff, exceeded by prominent, 3-toothed bracts**; produced in April to May; mature in 1 season, then shed seeds and fall intact.

Where Found: Moist to very dry sites; foothills to subalpine; central BC and Alberta to New Mexico.

Notes: The thick bark can withstand low-intensity fires. These trees can survive for many years; some have been known to reach over 1,300 years of age. • The seeds were eaten by many tribes, and young twigs and needles were used to make tea. Under rare climatic conditions, a crystalline sugar appears on the branches in early summer. The Interior Salish people harvested this 'tree breast milk.' • Dried sap was chewed to relieve cold symptoms. • Douglas-fir boughs were often used for bedding. Rotted wood from old logs was burned slowly to smoke hides. Because the wood is strong and durable, it provides excellent lumber, plywood, poles and railway ties. The resin was sometimes burned as a fumigant. The fragrant needles make Douglas-fir popular as a Christmas tree. • The 3-toothed bracts that project out past the scales have been likened to the tails and hind legs of mice. A Blackfoot story tells how the mice ran into the cones to hide from Naapi (a legendary character). • Many birds and small mammals eat the abundant seeds. Mule deer often rely on these trees for food and shelter in winter. • The name *Pseudotsuga* was derived from the Latin *pseudo*, 'false,' and *Tsuga*, 'hemlock.'

WESTERN HEMLOCK
Tsuga heterophylla

General: Coniferous, evergreen tree, usually 30–50 m tall; trunk straight, up to 1 m in diameter; **branches** slender, **down-swept**, appearing **feathery**; crown open, pyramidal, with a **flexible, nodding tip**.

Bark: Reddish-brown when young, becoming dark greyish-brown with age and developing deep furrows and flat ridges, thin, scaly; **inner bark dark orange with purple streaks**.

Leaves: Flat, evergreen **needles, 8–20 mm long**, of **unequal lengths**, blunt, yellowish-green, **arranged in 2 opposite rows**, on small stubs.

Cones: Male and female cones on same tree; pollen (male) cones 3–4 mm long, yellowish; seed (female) cones oblong–**egg-shaped, 15–25 mm long, hanging**, purplish-green when young, light brown when mature; scales thin, wavy-edged; produced in May to June; mature in 1 year, shed intact.

Where Found: Moist sites; foothills to montane; BC and Alberta to Idaho and Montana.

Notes: Mountain hemlock (***T. mertensiana***) has cones that are 2–3 times as long as those of western hemlock, and its leaves are in a spiral (bottlebrush-like) arrangement, not in 2 opposite rows. It grows mainly in the subalpine zone from southern BC to northern Idaho and Montana. • The boughs were used for bedding and as a disinfectant and deodorizer. • The hard, strong wood, with its even grain and colour, is widely used to make doors, windows, staircases, mouldings, cupboards and floors, and it also provides construction lumber, pilings, poles, railway ties, pulp and alpha cellulose for making paper, cellophane and rayon. • This attractive, feathery tree is a popular ornamental. Several cultivars have been developed. • Western hemlock is also known as Pacific hemlock and West Coast hemlock. The crushed needles were thought to smell like herbaceous hemlock plants, hence the common name. The species name *heterophylla* from the Latin *hetero*, 'variable,' and *phyllum,* 'leaf,' refers to the variably sized needles.

T. heterophylla

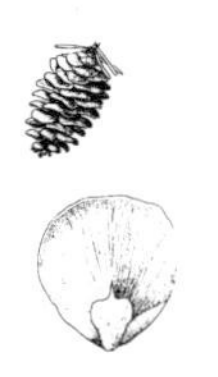

T. mertensiana

WESTERN RED CEDAR
Thuja plicata

General: Coniferous tree, to 40 m tall; trunk **straight, vertically lined, grey, buttressed at base**, 1–3 m in diameter; **branches spreading to hanging** but upturned at tips; crown cone-shaped when young, irregular with age.

Bark: Thin, cinnamon to greyish, easily peeled off in long, fibrous strips.

Leaves: Opposite, evergreen, **scale-like**, overlapping, about 3 mm long, **shiny, yellowish-green**, aromatic; arranged in 4 rows with upper/lower pair **flattened** and side pair folded, **in flat, fan-like sprays**.

Cones: Male and female cones on same tree in clusters at branch tips; pollen (male) cones almost round, about 2 mm long; seed (female) cones narrowly egg-shaped, 8–12 mm long, with **6–8 dry, brown scales**; produced April to May.

Where Found: Rich, moist to wet (often saturated) sites; foothills to montane; BC and western Alberta to Idaho and northwestern Montana.

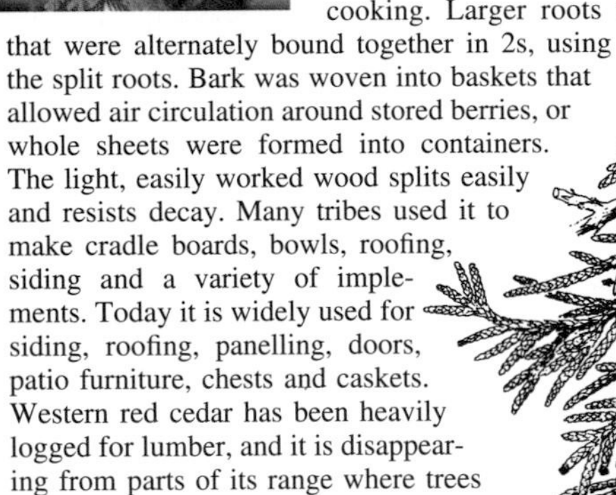

Notes: Western red cedar is very shade tolerant, but it has a low resistance to drought and frost. Its presence indicates relatively wet regions in the Rockies. In BC, this tree can reach over 1,000 years of age. • Bough tea was used to cure coughs and colds, often with honey added for children. Leaf tea was sometimes used to treat diarrhea. Native peoples twisted, wove and plaited the long, soft strips of inner bark to make a wide range of items, including baskets, blankets, clothing, ropes and mats. Dugout canoes, rafts and frames for birch bark canoes were made from the trunks. Fine roots were split and peeled to make water–tight baskets for cooking. Larger roots were formed into coils that were alternately bound together in 2s, using the split roots. Bark was woven into baskets that allowed air circulation around stored berries, or whole sheets were formed into containers. The light, easily worked wood splits easily and resists decay. Many tribes used it to make cradle boards, bowls, roofing, siding and a variety of implements. Today it is widely used for siding, roofing, panelling, doors, patio furniture, chests and caskets. Western red cedar has been heavily logged for lumber, and it is disappearing from parts of its range where trees have not been replanted. • The species name *plicata* means 'folded,' in reference to the flattened, overlapping leaves.

WESTERN LARCH
Larix occidentalis

General: Slender, coniferous tree, usually 25–50 m tall; trunk straight, usually 1–1.3 m in diameter; **branches short, well spaced with sparse leaves**; young twigs usually hairless; crown pyramid-like.

Bark: Cinnamon-brown, becoming 10–15 cm thick, deeply furrowed with large scales, similar to that of ponderosa pine.

Leaves: Tufts of 15–30 soft, 3-sided, **deciduous needles** on stubby twigs, 2.5–5 cm long, pale yellow-green in spring and summer, bright yellow in fall, shed for winter.

Cones: Male and female cones on same tree; pollen (male) cones yellow, about 1 cm long; seed (female) cones brown, egg-shaped, 2.5–4 cm long, with **scales wider than long and slender, 3-pointed bracts** projecting beyond scales; produced from May to June, mature in 1 season.

Where Found: Moist to dry, often gravelly or sandy sites; upper foothills to montane; BC and southwestern Alberta to Oregon and northwestern Montana.

Notes: Subalpine larch (*L. lyallii*) can be distinguished by its long-hairy, young twigs and its 4-sided needles. Generally, it grows at higher elevations, but when populations of these 2 species overlap, they can hybridize. Subalpine larch grows on rocky, exposed slopes near timberline, from BC and Alberta to Oregon and Montana. • Once or twice a year, the Flathead and Kutenai hollowed out a cavity in a western larch trunk, allowing about 4 litres of sweet syrup to accumulate. This substance could be evaporated to make it even sweeter, but some warned that eating too much 'cleans you out.' The sweet inner bark was eaten in spring and lumps of pitch were chewed like gum year-round. The sap and gum contain galatan, a natural sugar with a flavour like slightly bitter honey. Larch gum was also used as baking powder. • Larch gum was applied to cuts and bruises or chewed to relieve sore throats. Bark tea was taken to treat tuberculosis, colds and coughs. • The wood was used for making bowls, and rotted logs were collected for smoking buckskins. Today, it is often used in heavy construction, and it also makes good firewood. Arabino galatin, a water-soluble gum, is extracted from the bark for use in paint, ink and medicines. • The Kutenai chose the larch for their centre pole in the Sundance, whereas tribes further east chose the cottonwood. • Western larch is shade intolerant, and it has adapted to live in areas where forest fires are frequent. Mature trees have thick bark and few lower limbs; as a result they are able to survive low intensity fires, sometimes living for 700–900 years. Larch seeds germinate readily, and young trees grow rapidly on fire-blackened soils, but fire suppression and selective cutting have reduced populations in many areas. • The twigs are occasionally eaten by deer, and blue and spruce grouse eat the needles. • Western larch is also known as western tamarack, hackmatack and mountain larch. Lewis and Clark first described it in 1806 and Thomas Nuttall named it in 1849.

L. occidentalis

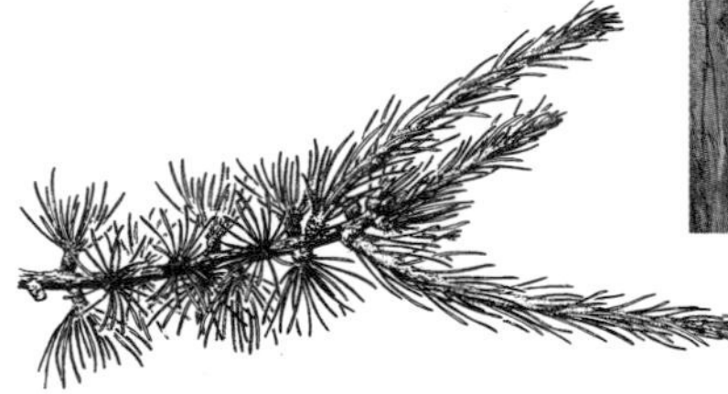

L. lyallii

LODGEPOLE PINE
Pinus contorta

General: Coniferous, evergreen tree, 20–35 m tall; trunk straight, largely bare of branches in closed stands; branches usually curved upwards; **crown open, pyramidal**.

Bark: Orange-brown to greyish, thin, scaly.

Leaves: Evergreen needles in **bundles of 2, 2–6 cm long, stiff**, often curved and twisted, deep green to yellow-green, lives 5–9 years.

Cones: Male and female cones on same tree; pollen (male) cones 8–10 mm long, reddish to yellowish-green, produced in spring at branch tips; seed (female) cones egg-shaped, **often asymmetrical, 2–6 cm long, spreading or bent backwards on branch**, green when young, brown when mature; scales thick, with a stiff prickle near tip; mature in 2 years and remain on branches for many years, some open to shed seeds, but many remain closed; produced in April to June.

Where Found: Moist to dry sites; foothills to montane; Alaska to Colorado.

Notes: In late spring and early summer, greenish-yellow clouds of pollen can fill the air, often landing on water, where it forms a yellow scum on quiet pools along shores. People with pollen allergies do not usually react strongly to pine pollen. • Lodgepole pine is a relatively short-lived tree (seldom over 200 years old) that thrives in areas that are periodically burned by forest fires. Although these thin-barked trees are easily killed by fire, their cones require heat to melt the resin that seals their scales shut. Following a fire, huge amounts of stock-piled seed are released, producing dense stands of young trees. These stands ('dog-hair stands') sometimes have over 100,000 trees per hectare. Older trees (100–140 years old) are more susceptible to disease and insect infestations—especially mountain pine beetle attacks. Extensive outbreaks can occur in mature, even-aged stands, and the dead trees provide fuel for forest fires, which begin the cycle again. • The inner bark is succulent and sweet in May and June (when the sap is running), and it was eaten or chewed like gum. Because it is difficult to digest raw, it was usually boiled; too much caused a bellyache. The nourishing seeds were also eaten. Evergreen tea is high in vitamin C, and was taken in winter to prevent or cure scurvy. It is still enjoyed today, often sweetened with sugar, honey, molasses or maple syrup, or spiced with cinnamon, nutmeg and orange peel. Evergreen teas should always be used in moderation, because **large amounts can be toxic. Pregnant women should not drink this tea.** • The inner bark was used as a dressing for scalds, burns and skin infections. The gummy sap (pitch) was chewed to soothe sore throats and to sweeten bad breath, and it was taken internally to treat kidney disorders and tuberculosis. Heated sap was applied to relieve sore muscles, arthritic joints, swellings and skin infections. Heated until it turned black, it was mixed with 1 part bone marrow to 4 parts sap, molded into cakes, and used as a poultice on burns. A poultice of sap, red axle grease and Climax chewing tobacco was used for boils! • The straight, slender trunks were historically used as poles in the construction of travois and tipis—hence the name 'lodgepole pine.' Each tipi required 25–30 poles, each 7–8 m long. These poles usually had to be replaced almost every year, and native peoples from the plains sometimes travelled 100s of miles to get new poles from the mountains. The wood is light-coloured and straight-grained, with a soft, even texture. In the past, it was used for making spears. Today the lumber is used to frame homes and construct mouldings and furniture. • Lodgepole pine is the official tree of Alberta. • This species is also known as black pine, scrub pine and mountain pine. The name 'jack pine' refers to the closely related species, *P. banksiana*, which grows east of the Rockies. Lodgepole pine was first described from specimens on the California coast, and the species name *contorta* refers to the twisted trees typical of that area; it has little to do with the straight-stemmed specimens of the mountains.

LIMBER PINE
Pinus flexilis

General: Coniferous, evergreen tree, 4–15 m tall, **often gnarled and twisted** on exposed sites; trunk short and stout, 35–60 cm in diameter; **branches thick, in whorls, plume-like**, often long and hanging with up-turned tips.

Bark: Light grey and smooth when young, dark brown and cracked with age, 2–5 cm thick.

Leaves: Evergreen **needles in bundles of 5**, dark yellowish-green, **4–7 cm long**, 3-sided, smooth-edged, stiff, slightly curved, crowded at branch tips.

Cones: Male and female cones on same tree; pollen (male) cones reddish, often conspicuous in spring at base of new growth; seed (female) cones light green when young, light brown at maturity, **oblong–egg-shaped, 5–12 cm long, short-stalked; scales thick but lacking prickles**; seeds large (about 1 cm long), essentially wingless, dark-mottled; mature in second year, open in autumn and fall during winter.

Where Found: Warm ridges and rocky slopes; foothills to subalpine; southern BC and Alberta to New Mexico.

Notes: The leaves, seeds and general appearance of **whitebark pine** (***P. albicaulis***) (bottom photo) resemble those of limber pine, but the purplish-brown cones of whitebark pine are only 1/2–1/3 as long as those of limber pine, and fall to the ground intact. Whitebark pine grows on exposed slopes near timberline from southern BC and Alberta to Wyoming. • **Western white pine** (***P. monticola***) is another '5-needled' pine that grows on rocky slopes in southern BC, Alberta and Montana. It is distinguished by its thin-scaled, long-stalked, cylindrical cones, and by its soft, finely toothed needles. • **Bristlecone pine** (***P. aristata***) has short (usually less than 4 cm long), strongly curved, sticky needles in groups of 5 that densely cover young branches, giving them a bottlebrush-like appearance. The scales of its cones are tipped with long prickles, hence the common name 'bristlecone pine.' It grows on dry and rocky sites in montane and subalpine zones in Colorado and New Mexico. • The slow-growing, frost-hardy, drought-resistant trees of limber pine and bristlecone pine are extremely long lived, surviving for well over 1,000 years. They often become dwarfed and twisted on exposed slopes. Several cultivars, including a dwarf form, are used as ornamental trees. The red clusters of pollen-bearing cones are conspicuous in spring. • The oil-rich, nutritious seeds were eaten by native peoples and early settlers, however, the cones of whitebark pine were generally considered too small and too 'greasy' to warrant the effort necessary. The cones were burned in a large fire, which cooked and released the seeds at the same time, and the seeds were then stored for later use. • The Navajo burned limber pine to produce 'good luck' smoke for hunters. They also used the needles to treat fevers and coughs. • The seeds of both limber and whitebark pine are eaten by many birds, small mammals and grizzly bears. Clark's nutcrackers are important in dispersing the heavy seeds, because they hide caches on windswept, south-facing slopes where there is little snow accumulation. Tree location may reflect the activities of the birds, rather than the site preferences of the trees. • Whitebark pine cones fall to the ground intact, but they are seldom found because birds, rodents and grizzly bears seek them out for their seeds • Limber pine is also called Rocky Mountain white pine. • The species name *flexilis* means 'pliant' or 'bendable,' in reference to the flexible branches, a necessary adaptation for survival under such windy and snowy conditions.

P. monticola

P. albicaulis

PONDEROSA PINE
Pinus ponderosa

General: Coniferous, evergreen tree, 10–40 m tall (sometimes up to 60 m); trunk straight, 1–1.5 m in diameter; branches numerous, stout, lower ones often drooping; crown open, irregularly cylindrical, often flat-topped.

Bark: Orange-brown to cinnamon with deep, black fissures delineating flat, flaky, **jigsaw-like plates**, up to 10 cm thick.

Leaves: Evergreen needles in **bundles of 3** (sometimes in 2s, 4s or 5s), yellow-green, **slender, 10–25 cm long**.

Cones: Male and female cones on same tree; pollen (male) cones 2–3 cm long, reddish-purple to yellow; **seed (female) cones broadly egg-shaped, 8–14 cm long in groups of 1–3**, reddish-purple when young, dull brown when mature; scales thick, with a **stiff prickle near tip**; mature in 2 years, then open and drop.

Where Found: Dry sites; foothills to montane; from southern BC to New Mexico.

Notes: In dry regions from Utah south, the large, oily seeds of **two-needle piñon (*P. edulis*)** were eagerly sought by native tribes and wildlife alike for food. Two-needle piñon is recognized by its dark green needles in bundles of 2, and its short (2.5–5 cm), thornless cones with 2 wingless, 1 cm long nutlets per scale. It is one of the most common trees in New Mexico. • Ponderosa pine trees thrive in areas that are periodically burned. Thick bark and bare lower trunks help mature trees to survive low-intensity fires, but they seldom live for more than 500 years. Douglas-fir (p. 30) and true firs (p. 27) are more tolerant of shady conditions, and they have replaced ponderosa pine in areas where fires have been suppressed for many years. Like lodgepole pine (p. 34), ponderosa pine is also susceptible to infestation by the mountain pine beetle. • The pale, older bark smells strongly like vanilla, especially on hot days. • The seeds are eaten by many birds and small mammals, including grouse, quail and squirrels. Porcupines eat the inner bark, and deer eat the twigs and needles. • The seeds were ground into meal and used to make bread. The sweet inner bark (said to taste something like sheep fat) was collected on cool, cloudy days when the sap was running. The bark was removed from one side of a tree (so as not to kill the tree), and the edible inner bark was then scraped from the tough outer layer. This was usually eaten immediately, but it could be kept moist, rolled in bags, for a few days. Some pines still bear large scars—telltale signs of early native peoples' fondness for pine cambium (inner bark). • Lumps of resin were chewed like gum. Resin was applied alone or in salves to boils, carbuncles, abscesses, rheumatic joints and aching backs. For dandruff, the pointed ends of the needles were jabbed into the scalp to 'kill the germs.' Pitch was chewed as gum, plastered in hair, used as glue, burned on torches, and used to waterproof woven containers. The light, soft wood was used to make dwellings, fence posts, saddle horns, snowshoes and baby cradles. Today, it is used as lumber and made into mouldings, cabinets and crates. • Ponderosa pine is also known as yellow pine, western yellow pine, bull pine and rock pine. The name 'ponderosa' was given to it because of its large size.

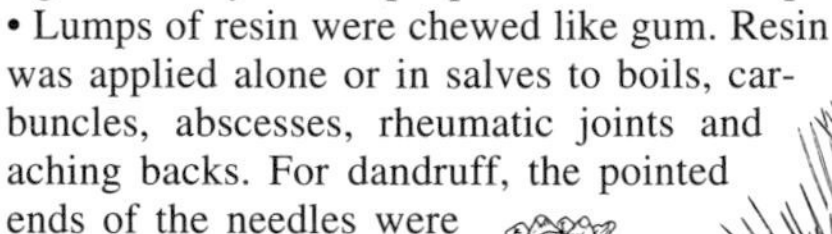

P. edulis

P. ponderosa

BALSAM POPLAR; BLACK COTTONWOOD
Populus balsamifera

General: Deciduous tree, 10–25 m tall (sometimes to 60 m); trunks often over 1 m thick; **buds large, resinous and fragrant**; crown broad, rounded.

Bark: Greenish-grey and smooth when young, marked with rough, blackened spots and lines, **deeply furrowed and dark grey when old**.

Leaves: Alternate, **egg-shaped, 5–12 cm long**, sharp-pointed at tip, rounded to heart-shaped at base, finely round-toothed, **thick, dark green above, paler and finely veined beneath; stalks round**.

Flowers: Tiny, in long, slender, **loosely hanging clusters (catkins)**; male and female catkins on separate trees; male catkins 2–3 cm long; **female catkins 4–10 cm long**; April to May.

Fruits: Egg-shaped, green capsules, 5–8 mm long, in **hanging catkins**, split into 2–3 parts when ripe; seeds tiny, with a tuft of soft, white hairs at tip, often dispersed in **large, fluffy masses**.

Where Found: Moist to wet sites, often on river and lakeshores; foothills to subalpine; Alaska to Colorado.

Notes: This species includes ***P. trichocarpa***. Many taxonomists recognize 2 species or subspecies in this one: *P. balsamifera* is a smaller, northern tree (common in Alberta and to the north), whose catkins have 2-parted, hairless female capsules or 12–20-stamened male flowers; *P. trichocarpa* is a taller, southern tree (common from southern Alberta to Colorado), whose catkins have 3-parted, often hairy female capsules or 40–60-stamened male flowers. • **Narrow-leaved cottonwood** (***P. angustifolia***) has slender, lance-shaped leaves that are 3–5 times longer than wide, with wedge-shaped bases and short (less than 1/3 as long as blade) stalks. Its buds are sticky and aromatic, and the capsules split into 2 parts when mature. It grows along rivers and streams in foothills and montane zones from southern Alberta and Idaho to New Mexico. • Many tribes relished the sweet inner bark of balsam poplar in spring, when the sap was running. After the thick outer bark had been removed, the translucent inner bark (cambium) could be scraped off. Sometimes, hollows were carved in trunks to collect sap. • The leaves were applied to bruises, sores, boils, aching muscles and sores on horses, which had become infected with maggots. Bark tea was said to be slightly **poisonous**, but it was used to treat tuberculosis and whooping cough, with each dose followed by cups of warm water. Cottonwood bark was chewed to relieve colds. • Balsam poplar wood was said to be ideal for tipi fires, because it did not crackle and it made clean smoke. In spring, buds mixed with blood produced a permanent black ink that was used to paint records on robes. Twigs and bark were occasionally fed to horses when forage was limited. When stealing horses, war parties carried balsam poplar bark with them to feed the horses and to mask human scent. Some warriors rubbed themselves with the sap. • These trees produce millions of tiny, fragile seeds with fluffy tufts of hairs to carry them on the wind. Cottonwoods can also re-sprout from stumps and branches and grow from rhizomes. The thick, deeply fissured bark of mature trees protects them from fires. • Moose and other ungulates browse on young balsam poplar trees. In spring, bees collect the sticky, aromatic resin from the buds and young leaves, and use it to cement and waterproof their hives.

P. angustifolia

P. balsamifera

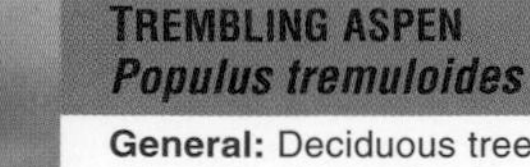

TREMBLING ASPEN
Populus tremuloides

General: Deciduous tree, 10–20 m tall (sometimes to 30 m); trunk slender; branches fairly short; **buds small, not resinous or fragrant**; crown short, rounded.

Bark: Greenish-white, smooth, marked with rough, blackened spots and lines, also black and rough on lower trunk.

Leaves: Alternate, **oval to round, 2–8 cm long**, pointed at tip, finely round-toothed; **stalks long, slender, flattened**, allowing leaves to tremble with light breezes.

Flowers: Tiny, in dense, long, slender, **loosely hanging clusters (catkins)**; male and female catkins on separate trees, 2–10 cm long; March to May.

Fruits: Cone-shaped capsules, 3–6 mm long, in hanging catkins; seeds tiny, with a tuft of soft hairs at tip.

Where Found: Dry to moist sites; foothills to subalpine; Alaska to New Mexico.

Notes: This sun-loving tree often colonizes slopes that have been burned or logged, re-sprouting from shallow roots. Female trees can produce millions of seeds each year, which are carried to new sites by the wind. These seeds live for only a short time, and seldom germinate (although recent fires in Yellowstone resulted in a burst of aspen regeneration by seed). Usually trembling aspen reproduces by sending up suckers from its extensive, shallow root systems. This process can produce stands of trees called 'clones,' in which all of the trees are connected underground and all are genetically identical. These clones can cover several hectares, surviving for 1,000s of years. The extent of a clone is often seen most clearly in spring, when all of its trees break bud together, and again in autumn, when they all turn yellow and drop their leaves at the same time. • In spring when the sap began to flow, the sweet, pulpy inner bark was considered a treat for children of some northern tribes. It was scraped off in long strips and eaten raw. • Bark tea was used to treat ruptures, but the bark had to be collected by stripping it downwards from the tree; otherwise the patient would vomit it out! Traditionally, herbalists used aspen bark to treat intermittent fevers and urinary tract infections, to cure jaundice, debility and diarrhea, and to kill parasitic worms. • Aspen wood was used to make paddles and bowls. The trunks were used as tipi poles. In spring, when the bark can be slid from the branches, short sections can be used to make toy whistles. Today, aspen wood is harvested for pulp, and it is also used to make chopsticks. Because it does not splinter, aspen wood is preferred for sauna benches and playground equipment. • The greenish bark of these trees is photosynthetic. Sometimes it produces a white powdery material for protection from ultraviolet radiation, and in exposed sites trunks can become so white that from a distance the trees are mistaken for white birch. This powder rubs off easily, and natives are said to have used it for sunscreen. • Aspen is an attractive, fast-growing tree, but it is seldom used in landscaping; it is susceptible to many diseases and insects, and its spreading root systems tend to grow where they are not wanted (invading sewers and drainpipes). • Trembling aspen is the preferred food and building material of beavers. Deer and elk eat the twigs and leaves, and in times of famine, some even eat the bark, leaving extensive black scars on the trunks up to about 2 m from the ground. Old aspen trees are very susceptible to rot, and many birds and small mammals nest in their cavities. • Trembling aspen is also known as quaking aspen, golden aspen, mountain aspen, popple, poplar and trembling poplar. Two native names translate as 'woman's tongue' and 'noisy leaf.'

WHITE BIRCH; PAPER BIRCH
Betula papyrifera

General: Deciduous tree, 10–20 m tall; trunk to 75 cm in diameter, **often with several trunks** from a branching base; branches slender, sometimes with crystalline glands near tips.

Bark: White to yellowish or sometimes brownish, marked with brown, horizontal lines of raised pores, smooth, peeling in **papery** sheets; fissured and black at base of older trees.

Leaves: Alternate, egg-shaped, 4–9 cm long (sometimes to 10 cm), **slender-pointed**, sharply irregular- or double-toothed, pale green, yellow in autumn.

Flowers: Tiny, in dense, long, slender clusters (catkins), male and female flowers in separate catkins on same tree; pollen (male) catkins 5–10 cm long, loosely hanging; **seed (female) catkins 2–4 cm long, erect at maturity, eventually shed nutlets and 3-lobed scales**, leaving only a slender central stalk; April to May.

Fruits: Winged, oval nutlets, 2 mm long; **wings broader than nutlets**; shed in fall and winter.

Where Found: Open to dense, dry to moist sites; foothills to subalpine; Alaska to Colorado.

Notes: Water birch (*B. occidentalis*), also known as **mountain birch**, is a smaller tree, with dark, tight bark that does not peel. Its leaves are smaller (2–4.5 cm long) with abruptly pointed (not tapered) tips. It grows along streams and lakeshores in foothills, montane and subalpine zones from Alaska to northern New Mexico. When the ranges of water birch and white birch overlap, these 2 species often hybridize. • Paper birch thrives in open sites, but rarely lives for more than 140 years. It re-sprouts readily after fire or browsing, producing clumps of trees. • Birch sap, collected during spring flow, can be boiled to make a syrup (similar to maple syrup). This sap has also been used to make beer, wine and soft drinks. • Recent research indicates that betulic acid (the compound that makes birch bark white) may be useful for treating skin cancer. It could become an ingredient in future sunscreens and tanning lotions. • The thin, paper-like bark of these trees was widely used by native peoples to make canoes, baskets, storage containers, cups and platters. Thin strips of bark make excellent kindling, and the wood produces long-burning, sweet-smelling fires. The wood is very hard, and was fashioned into sleds, snowshoes, paddles, canoe ribs, arrows, tool handles and even needles. Birch trunks were sometimes used as poles for making tipis and drying racks. **Do not collect birch bark from living trees**; bark removal can permanently scar and even kill birches. • Deer and moose eat the leaves and twigs, and many small birds feed on the seeds. • White birch is also called canoe birch and silver birch.

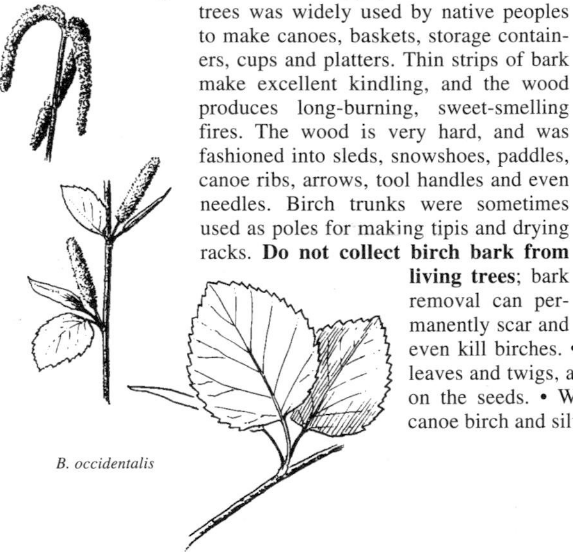

B. occidentalis

SHRUBS

Shrubs are woody plants that are usually multi-stemmed and less than 10 m tall when mature. Rocky Mountain shrubs include a wide variety of plant families and genera; we have organized them by major plant families and by similar species within these families. This section contains a key to shrub genera and keys to species for some of the larger genera (*Ribes*, *Vaccinium*, *Salix*).

Key to Shrub Genera

1a. Plants inconspicuous, yellowish-green, fleshy, parasitic shrubs, with segmented stems, growing on tree branches .... ***Arceuthobium*** (p. 46)

1b. Plants larger, free-living shrubs growing from the ground, with green (photosynthetic) leaves 2

2a. Leaves needle- or scale-like, evergreen 3

3a. Tall shrubs or small trees, 5–10 m tall; leaves needle-like; fruit a bluish seed surrounded by a fleshy, scarlet cup, berry-like .... ***Taxus*** (p. 48)

3b. Small shrubs (usually less than 1 m tall; if taller [*Juniperus scopulorum*], leaves scale-like); fruit not as above 4

4a. Leaves opposite or in whorls of 3 5

5a. Fruits bluish, berry-like cones; leaves needle- or scale-like; shrubs often pungent; low elevations to subalpine (occasionally alpine) .... ***Juniperus*** (p. 47)

5b. Fruits round capsules; leaves scale-like; plants not strong smelling; subalpine to alpine .... ***Cassiope*** (p. 76)

4b. Leaves alternate (sometimes in whorls of 4 in *Empetrum*) 6

6a. Leaves 5–12 mm long; fruits round capsules .... ***Phyllodoce*** (p. 77)

6b. Leaves 3–7 mm long; fruits juicy black 'berries' .... ***Empetrum*** (see *Phyllodoce*, p. 77)

2b. Leaves usually broad and flat, not needle- or scale-like 7

7a. Stems with spines or prickles 8

8a. Leaves compound (divided into leaflets); fruits red 9

9a. Flowers pink; fruits 'hips' .... ***Rosa*** (p. 68)

9b. Flowers white; fruits raspberries .... ***Rubus*** (p. 67)

8b. Leaves not divided into leaflets (but sometimes lobed) 10

10a. Leaves large (10–40 cm wide) and spiny .... ***Oplopanax*** (p. 59)

10b. Leaves not spiny and usually smaller 11

11a. Leaves deeply 3–5-lobed (somewhat like a maple leaf); fruits reddish to purplish-black berries .... ***Ribes*** (p. 56)

11b. Leaves not lobed, or very shallowly lobed at tip; fruits various 12

12a. Shrubs 100–400 cm tall; leaves 3–6 cm long; fruits fleshy pomes (like tiny apples) .... ***Crataegus*** (p. 63)

12b. Shrubs 10–50 cm tall; leaves 1–3 cm long; fruits dry, 3-lobed capsules .... ***Ceanothus fendleri*** .... (see *C. velutinus*, p. 70)

7b. Stems lacking spines and prickles 13

13a. Flowers and fruits in catkins (spikes of tiny flowers, often resembling caterpillars when mature) 14

14a. Buds enclosed in a single bud scale .... ***Salix*** (p. 49)

14b. Buds enclosed in 2 or more scales 15

15a. Bark has horizontal markings of raised pores (lenticels); leaves roundish; fruiting catkins neither woody nor persistent; pith usually flattened in cross-section; no bud at stem tip .... ***Betula*** (p. 55)

15b. Bark usually lacks lenticel markings; leaves oval to elliptic; fruiting catkins woody, persistent 'cones'; pith usually 3-sided in cross-section; bud at stem tip .... ***Alnus*** (p. 55)

13b. Flowers and fruits not in catkins 16

16a. Bark has horizontal markings (lenticels); flowers white, fragrant; fruits red to purplish-black cherries .... ***Prunus*** (p. 65)

16b. Bark lacks lenticel markings; flowers and fruits various 17

17a. Leaves opposite or in whorls 18

18a. Leaves in whorls of 3–8 .... ***Chimaphila*** (p. 78)

18b. Leaves opposite 19

19a. Leaves evergreen, leathery 20

20a. Plants 5–20 cm tall; leaves not toothed, the edges are rolled under; flowers rose-pink, 2–12 mm across .... ***Kalmia*** (p. 76)

20b. Plants 20–60 cm tall; leaves sharply toothed; flowers greenish-brown to dark reddish, 3–4 mm across .... ***Paxistima*** (p. 74)

19b. Leaves deciduous 21

21a. Young stems usually bright red; leaves have 5–7 prominent, nearly parallel veins that converge at tip .... ***Cornus*** (p. 71)

21b. Young stems not bright red; leaves have branching veins 22

22a. Leaves pinnately compound with 5–9 leaflets per leaf 23

23a. Tall shrubs or small trees (to 12 m tall); leaves with 3–5 leaflets; fruits V-shaped pairs of winged seeds (samaras) ...***Acer negundo*** (see *A. glabrum*, p. 59)

23b. Smaller shrubs (to 3 m tall); leaves with 5–7 leaflets; fruits red, purple or black, berry-like .... ***Sambucus*** (p. 60)

22b. Leaves simple (not divided into leaflets) 24

24a. Leaves 3-lobed 25
25a. Large shrubs or small trees to 10 m tall; flowers pale yellowish-green; fruits V-shaped pairs of winged seeds (samaras) .... ***Acer*** (p. 59)
25b. Medium-sized shrubs to 4 m tall; flowers white; fruits red or orange berries .... ***Viburnum*** (p. 60)
24b. Leaves oval to elliptic, not lobed 26
26a. Flowers inconspicuous, less than 4 mm across, yellowish-brown, lacking petals; branches and leaves with brown scabs or scales .... ***Shepherdia*** (p. 73)
26b. Flowers showier, more than 5 mm across, with petals; branches and leaves neither scaly nor scabby 27
27a. Flowers white, cross-shaped, fragrant .... ***Philadelphus*** (p. 72)
27b. Flowers bell-shaped to tubular, not strongly sweet-smelling.. 28
28a. Flowers bluish-lavender to pale purple, in pairs or short clusters at branch tips .... ***Penstemon*** (p. 62)
28b. Flowers white to pink, yellow, orange or red 29
29a. Flowers usually less than 1 cm long, bell- or urn-shaped, white to pink; fruits white berries that remain through winter .... ***Symphoricarpos*** (p. 61)
29b. Flowers usually more than 1 cm long, tubular, yellow to orange; fruits red, blue or purplish-black berries that do not remain through winter .... ***Lonicera*** (p. 61)
17b. Leaves alternate 30
30a. Leaves evergreen, often leathery 31
31a. Leaves pinnately compound, edged with spine-tipped teeth (holly-like) ...... ***Mahonia*** (p. 69)
31b. Leaves simple (not divided into leaflets), not edged with spine-tipped teeth 32
32a. Plants trailing or creeping, less than 20 cm tall 33
33a. Petals bent backwards sharply (like miniature shootingstar-like flowers); leaves widely spaced
.... ***Oxycoccos* spp.**
.... (see *Gaultheria*, p. 78)
33b. Flowers urn- or bell-shaped; leaves not widely spaced 34
34a. Fruits white or red berries; plants with mild wintergreen odour ...... ***Gaultheria*** (p. 78)
34b. Fruits red berries; plants lacking wintergreen odour 34
35a. Leaves with dark dots on underside; often found on moist to wet sites .... ***Vaccinium vitis-idaea***
.... (see *Vaccinium scoparium*, p. 79)
35b. Leaves lacking dark dots on underside; usually found on well-drained sites ...... ***Arctostaphylos*** (p. 77)

32b. Plants upright, usually more than 20 cm tall 36

36a. Plants small (5–25 cm tall) but upright, with showy clusters of bright rose-purple flowers; alpine .... ***Rhododendron lapponicum*** .... (see *R. albiflorum*, p. 81)

36b. Plants larger (generally more than 30 cm tall); flowers not as above; low elevations to subalpine 37

37a. Leaves 4–8 cm long, shiny and often sticky above ...... ***Ceanothus velutinus*** (p. 80)

37b. Leaves 1.5–4 cm long, not shiny or sticky above 38

38a. Shrubs greyish; leaves mainly wedge-shaped; dry plains and slopes .... ***Artemisia*** (p. 74)

38b. Shrubs green; leaves elliptic to oval; moist to wet, open or wooded sites .... ***Ledum*** (p. 75)

30b. Leaves deciduous, usually thin 39

39a. Leaves compound (divided into leaflets) 40

40a. Flowers small, cream-coloured to greenish-yellow; fruits berry-like drupes, 4–7 mm long 41

41a. Leaves with 3 large (over 3 cm long) leaflets, often causing severe skin reactions; fruits white or yellowish-white, smooth drupes .... ***Toxicodendron*** (p. 72)

41b. Leaves pinnately compound or with 3 small (less than 3 cm long) leaflets, not causing skin reactions; fruits orange or red, fuzzy drupes .... ***Rhus*** (p. 71)

40b. Flowers showier, white or bright yellow; fruits berry-like pomes (7–8 mm long) or seed-like 42

42a. Leaflets 7–13; flowers white, in dense clusters; fruits red pomes .... ***Sorbus*** (p. 69)

42b. Leaflets 3–7; flowers yellow, single; fruits seed-like .... ***Pentaphylloides*** (p. 68)

39b. Leaves simple (not divided into leaflets) 43

43a. Leaves deeply lobed, generally oak- or maple-leaf–shaped 44

44a. Leaves oak-shaped; fruits acorns .... ***Quercus*** .... (see *Acer glabrum,* p. 59)

44b. Leaves maple-leaf–shaped; fruits not acorns 45

45a. Bark brown, shredding; fruits egg-shaped pairs of capsules ....***Physocarpus*** (p. 63)

45b. Bark not shredding; fruits not pairs of capsules 46

46a. Fruits shallowly domed clusters of red drupelets, like squashed raspberries; flowers white, showy, 2.5–5 cm across .... ***Rubus parviflorus*** (p. 67)

46b. Fruits reddish to black berries; flowers various colours, less showy, usually less than 1 cm across .... ***Ribes*** (p. 56)

43b. Leaves not lobed (sometimes shallowly lobed in *Holodiscus*, p. 66) 47

47a. Flowers tiny, in heads characteristic of the sunflower family (p. 215), with disk florets only, usually found on dry, open sites at lower elevations 48

48a. Leaves white-felted; flowerheads with 4–6 bracts .... ***Tetradymia*** .... (see *Chrysothamnus*, p. 75)

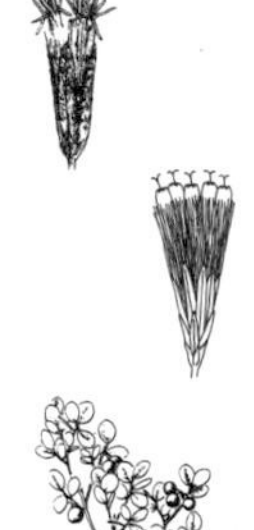

48b. Leaves grey-velvety; flowerheads with several rows of bracts .... ***Chrysothamnus*** (p. 75)

47b. Flowers of other types 49

49a. Flowers urn- to bell-shaped, white to pinkish or greenish-orange 50

50a. Fruits blue to blue-black berries; flowers white to pinkish .... ***Vaccinium*** (p. 79)

50b. Fruits dry, not berries; flowers peach-pink to green or greenish-orange 51

51a. Leaves elliptic, with midvein protruding at tip; fruits are capsules; moist, wooded sites; BC and Alberta to Wyoming .... ***Menziesia*** (p. 81)

51b. Leaves lance-shaped to rounded, midvein not protruding at tip; fruits seed-like, with long, feathery tails; open to fairly open sites; Montana to New Mexico .... ***Cercocarpus*** (p. 64)

49b. Flowers not urn- or bell-shaped, various colours 52

52a. Flowers white 53

53a. Flowers large (1.5–2 cm across) 54

54a. Leaves entire (not toothed); fruits woody capsules .... ***Rhododendron*** (p. 81)

54b. Leaves coarsely toothed on upper 1/2; fruits purple to black, berry-like pomes .... ***Amelanchier*** (p. 66)

53b. Flowers small (less than 1 cm across), many in large clusters 55

55a. Stems red; leaves sometimes shiny and sticky .... ***Ceanothus sanguineus*** .... (see *C. velutinus*, p. 70)

55b. Stems brownish; leaves never shiny and sticky 56

56a. Shrubs 40–70 cm tall; flowers in dense, flat-topped clusters 3–8 cm across .... ***Spiraea*** (p. 64)

56b. Shrubs 100–300 cm tall; flowers in feathery, 10–17 cm long, branched clusters .... ***Holodiscus*** (p. 66)

52b. Flowers yellow or yellowish-brown 57

57a. Leaves wedge-shaped, 3-toothed at tip .... ***Purshia*** .... (see *Artemisia tridentata*, p. 74)

57b. Leaves lance- to egg-shaped, finely toothed or toothless 58

58a. Twigs densely covered with rusty, brown scales; leaves silvery; fruits silvery berries .... ***Elaeagnus*** (p. 73)

58b. Twigs smooth or finely grey-hairy; leaves green; fruits bluish-black 'berries' 59

59a. Shrubs to 1.5 m tall; leaves with 5–7 side veins .... ***Rhamnus*** (p. 70)

59b. Shrubs or small trees to 10 m tall; leaves with 10–12 side veins .... ***Frangula*** .... (see *Rhamnus*, p. 70)

AMERICAN DWARF MISTLETOE
Arceuthobium americanum

General: Inconspicuous, yellowish-green, fleshy, parasitic shrub; visible stems usually tufted, 1–2 mm thick, 2–6 cm long (sometimes to 10 cm), **segmented**, with **whorled branches**; from extensive stems growing under bark of host tree.

Leaves: Opposite, reduced to **tiny scales**.

Flowers: Greenish-yellow, inconspicuous, male or female on 1 plant, with 2 (female flower) or 3 (male flower) tiny sepals and no petals; **few to several flowers in whorls** (female) **or branched clusters** (male); April to July.

Fruits: Sticky, egg-shaped berries, bluish-green to blue with a whitish cast, 2–3 mm long, short-stalked, nodding, explosively eject 1 sticky seed.

Where Found: Parasitic, exclusively on pines, usually on lodgepole pine (p. 34); foothills to montane; BC and Alberta to New Mexico.

Notes: Several species of dwarf mistletoe with flattened, fan-like branches grow on other trees in the Rocky Mountains. **Sheathed dwarf mistletoe** (***A. vaginatum***) is one of the most common in the southern Rockies, where it is often found growing on ponderosa pine (p. 36). It is a robust, yellowish species with branches 2–15 cm long and over 2 mm thick at their base. Its short, stout (3–4 mm wide) flower spikes appear in early summer. **Western dwarf mistletoe** (***A. campylopodum***) (lower photo) is an olive-green or brown plant with even stouter branches (over 3 mm thick) that flower in late autumn. It is found on a wide variety of hosts, including firs (p. 27), junipers (pp. 47–48), larches (p. 33), spruces (pp. 28–29) and pines (pp. 34–36), from BC and Alberta to New Mexico. Some taxonomists have divided western dwarf mistletoe into several species or forms, based on the host species. **Douglas' dwarf mistletoe** (***A. douglasii***) is a small, slender species with branches about 1 mm thick and seldom over 2 cm long. Its stems are scattered, rather than tufted, on the branches of Douglas-fir (p. 30), its only host, from BC and Alberta to New Mexico. • Dwarf mistletoe causes disorganized growth of pines, called 'witch's broom,' which can weaken and even kill the host tree. Although they can cause significant reductions in tree growth, dwarf mistletoes have coexisted with trees for 1000s of generations. These parasitic plants are extremely specialized, and many conifer species have their own species or race of *Arceuthobium*.

ROCKY MOUNTAIN JUNIPER
Juniperus scopulorum

General: Coniferous, evergreen **shrub to small tree**, usually erect, 1–10 m tall with an **irregularly rounded crown**; small branches slender, scaly, with overlapping leaves, **cedar-like**; trunks twisted, knotty, reddish-brown with narrow ridges of scaly or stringy bark.

Leaves: Opposite, in 4 vertical rows, lying flat against branch, barely overlapping, **scale-like**, 1–1.5 mm long, **greyish-green**; young leaves longer (5–7 mm) and needle-like.

Cones: Male and female cones on separate shrubs, scattered among leaves; pollen (male) cones egg-shaped, about 5 mm long; **seed (female) cones berry-like, bluish-purple**, often with a greyish bloom, round, usually 2-seeded; produced in May to June, seed cones mature in 2nd year.

Where Found: Dry, rocky, open sites; foothills to montane; BC and Alberta to New Mexico.

Notes: These seeds cannot germinate until the fleshy covering of the cones has been removed, which is usually accomplished by passage of the 'berries' through the digestive tract of a bird or mammal. Townsend's solitaires and bighorn sheep both feed on Rocky Mountain juniper. • These shrubs usually live for 200–300 years, but some can survive for up to 1,500 years. • This shrub should be treated with caution, because it can prove **toxic** (see notes under common juniper, p. 48). • These long-lived, evergreen shrubs represented youthfulness, and their needles were burned to provide sacred, purifying smoke to bring relief from colds (Sioux, Kutenai), ward off illness, and bring protection from witches, thunder and lightning (because lightning never strikes a juniper tree). If a horse was sick, it was made to inhale this smoke 3 times for a cure.

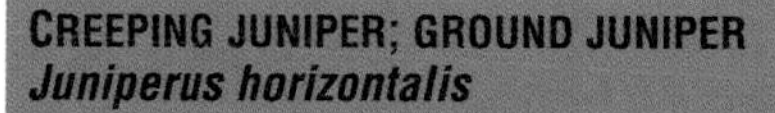

CREEPING JUNIPER; GROUND JUNIPER
Juniperus horizontalis

General: Prostrate, evergreen shrub, seldom over 15 cm high with long, trailing branches bearing many short side branches; **side branches slender, scaly with overlapping leaves, cedar-like**.

Leaves: Opposite, in 4 vertical rows, **lying flat** against branch, **scale-like**, 1–1.5 mm long, green to **greyish-green** or bluish.

Cones: Male and female cones on separate shrubs, scattered among leaves; pollen (male) cones egg-shaped, about 5 mm long; **seed (female) cones berry-like, bluish-purple** with a greyish bloom, about 6 mm long; produced in May to June, seed cones mature in the following year.

Where Found: Dry, rocky, open sites; plains to subalpine; the Yukon and NWT to Wyoming.

Notes: Rocky Mountain juniper and creeping juniper often hybridize when they grow in the same region. They grow in similar habitats, but Rocky Mountain juniper is more common in the southern US Rockies, whereas creeping juniper fills this niche further north. • Some tribes used creeping juniper berries to make medicinal teas for treating kidney problems, but this shrub should be treated with caution, because it can prove **toxic** (see notes under common juniper, p. 48). • The attractive, aromatic 'berries' were combined with wolfwillow seeds to make necklaces. The branches were burned as a smudge to repel insects. Both berries and branches were used in religious ceremonies by northern tribes.

COMMON JUNIPER
Juniperus communis

General: Coniferous, evergreen shrub, spreading, 30–100 cm tall; often forms **mats or clumps**.

Leaves: Mostly in whorls of 3, **sharp needles, 5–12 mm long**, whitish above, dark green beneath.

Cones: Male and female cones on separate shrubs, in clusters at branch tips; pollen (male) cones round to egg-shaped, about 3–5 mm long; **seed (female) cones berry-like, dark blue**, often with a greyish bloom, round, 8–12 mm long, with 3–8 fleshy scales; produced from April to May, seed cones mature in 2nd year.

Where Found: Dry, open sites or open forest; plains to alpine; Alaska to New Mexico.

Notes: People with kidney problems and pregnant women should never take any part of this plant internally. In Europe, an old name for juniper was 'bastard killer' because it was used to produce abortions, sometimes with **fatal** results for the woman. • This plant was not widely used by native peoples, but Europeans used the berry-like cones medicinally to make teas for aiding digestion and appetite, for stimulating sweating, urination and mucous secretion, for treating diarrhea, heart, lung and kidney problems, and (as a wash) for swelling and inflammation. The Blackfeet used juniper tea to treat lung and venereal diseases. Juniper needles were dried and powdered as a dusting for skin diseases. They were also boiled or burned like incense to purify homes and protect the inhabitants from disease and evil spirits. The Navajo burned juniper to make 'good luck' smoke for hunters. • The species name *communis* means 'common,' which this species is, over much of the globe. It is the only circumpolar conifer in the northern hemisphere.

WESTERN YEW
Taxus brevifolia

General: Evergreen shrub, spreading to erect, usually 2–10 m tall; trunks often twisted and/or clumped, **with dark reddish to purplish, papery outer bark and rose-coloured inner bark**; branches horizontal, drooping.

Leaves: Flat needles, 14–18 mm long, **pointed**, green on both sides, spirally arranged but twisted to form **2 opposite rows** along branches, persist 5–6 years.

Flowers: Tiny, in **very small cones about 2–3 mm long**, male or female with both sexes among the needles of separate trees; pollen (male) cones yellowish, round, tipped with a stalked cluster of pollen sacs; seed (female) cones with 1 ovule at tip; April to June.

Fruits: Scarlet, berry-like, with fleshy tissue (aril) around a single, bony seed, 4–5 mm across, open at 1 end (cup-like); September to October.

Where Found: Moist, shady sites; foothills to montane; BC and Alberta to Idaho and Montana.

Notes: The leaves, bark and seeds contain 'taxine,' a toxic alkaloid that is extremely **poisonous** and often **fatal** if ingested. • The bark of western yew is a source of 'taxol,' a drug used to treat ovarian cancer and breast cancer. Some native peoples used the bark for treating illness. • The heavy, fine-grained wood has been used to make bows, wedges, clubs, paddles, digging sticks, tool handles and harpoons. It is still prized today by carvers. The Flathead carved bows from seasoned yew wood and then varnished them with boiled animal sinew and muscle • Yews make good ornamental shrubs, but their berries, branches and leaves are **poisonous**, so they could be **dangerous** to children. • Many birds eat the fruits and disperse the seeds. Although this shrub is a preferred winter browse for moose, the leaves and branches are said to be poisonous to horses and cattle (especially if left to rot).

WILLOWS

Willows (*Salix* spp.) in the Rocky Mountains range from prostrate, dwarf shrubs to small trees. Individual species can be highly variable, and hybridization is common. Willows can be recognized by the single scale on each bud. They have tiny flowers in dense spikes (catkins), with male or female catkins on separate shrubs. Seeds, each with a tuft of cottony hair, are released to the wind from pointed capsules. Willow flowers and catkins are illustrated on p. 363.

Key to Willows (*Salix* Species)

1a. Plants dwarf, sometimes trailing, alpine shrubs less than 10 cm tall 2

- 2a. Mature leaves hairless beneath, usually strongly net-veined above, rounded or blunt at tip .... ***S. reticulata*** (see *S. arctica*, p. 51)
- 2b. Mature leaves usually hairy beneath (at least with a tuft of hair at tip), not net-veined above, sharply pointed at tip .... ***S. arctica*** (p. 51)

1b. Plants taller, erect shrubs or small trees 3

- 3a. Leaf edges toothed 4
  - 4a. Leaves hairy at maturity (at least beneath) 5
    - 5a. Leaf edges distantly toothed with short, slender projections; leaves linear, at least 10 times as long as wide; shrubs in colonies on floodplains .... ***S. exigua*** (see *S. myrtillifolia*, p. 52)
    - 5b. Leaf edges closely saw-toothed or scalloped; leaves not linear 6
      - 6a. Leaves soft hairy and prominently veined on lower surface (especially when young), egg-shaped, rounded at base; stalk of capsule 2–5 mm long .... ***S. bebbiana*** (see *S. glauca*, p. 53)
      - 6b. Leaves narrowly elliptical, tapered to stalk at base with short, stiff parallel hairs on lower surface, not prominently veined; stalk of capsule at most 1 mm long .... ***S. arbusculoides*** (see *S. scouleriana*, p. 53)
  - 4b. Leaves hairless, or inconspicuously hairy at maturity 7
    - 7a. Lower surface of leaves green, lacking a whitish bloom .... ***S. myrtillifolia*** (p. 52)
    - 7b. Lower surface of leaves with a whitish bloom 8
      - 8a. Capsules silky-hairy .... ***S. planifolia*** (p. 52)
      - 8b. Capsules hairless 9
        - 9a. Catkins stalkless, with no leafy bracts at base; unfolding leaves reddish .... ***S. monticola*** (see *S. planifolia*, p. 52)
        - 9b. Catkins on leafy stalks .... ***S. barclayi*** (see *S. planifolia*, p. 52)
- 3b. Leaf edges toothless or indistinctly toothed 10
  - 10a. Leaves hairless at maturity 11

11a. Stipules (especially on young, vigorous shoots) prominent .... ***S. barclayi*** (see *S. planifolia*, p. 52)

11b. Stipules inconspicuous or absent 12

12a. Male catkins about 1 cm long .... ***S. geyeriana*** (see *S. barrattiana*, p. 54)

12b. Male catkins 1.5–4 cm long 13

13a. Capsules with short hairs .... ***S. planifolia*** (p. 52)

13b. Capsules hairless .... ***S. farriae*** (see *S. planifolia*, p. 52)

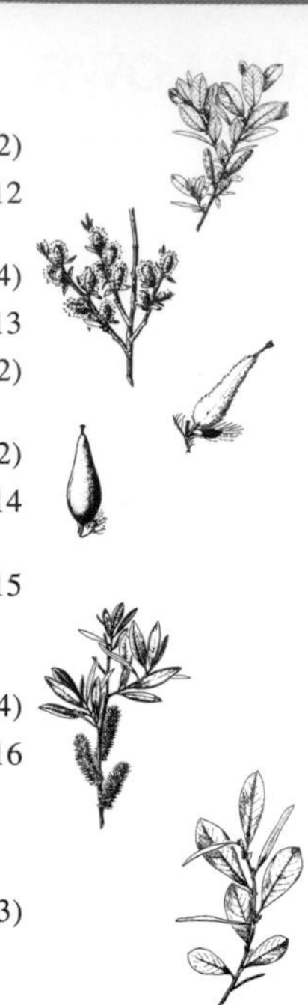

10b. Leaves distinctly hairy at maturity 14

14a. Lower surface of leaves densely and opaquely hairy 15

15a. Branchlets hairless, yellowish, with a pale greyish, waxy bloom .... ***S. drummondiana*** (see *S. barrattiana*, p. 54)

15b. Branchlets woolly, lacking a waxy bloom 16

16a. Leaf stalks velvety with erect hairs; lower leaf surface not white-woolly, bearing some straight, rust-coloured hairs .. ***S. scouleriana*** (p. 53)

16b. Leaf stalks woolly with matted hairs; lower leaf surface white woolly 17

17a. Shrubs 30–100 cm tall, growing at low to mid elevations; leaves 6–16 mm wide .... ***S. candida*** (p. 54)

17b. Shrubs 1–9 m tall, growing in subalpine to alpine zones; leaves 20–25 mm wide .... ***S. alaxensis*** .... (see *S. candida*, p. 54)

14b. Lower surface of leaves hairy, but leaf surface visible 18

18a. Lower surface of leaves green, without a whitish bloom .... ***S. commutata*** (see *S. myrtillifolia*, p. 52)

18b. Lower surface of leaves with a whitish bloom 19

19a. Leaf hairs rust-coloured, including some with matted hairs .... ***S. scouleriana*** (p. 53)

19b. Leaf hairs all white 20

20a. Catkins stalkless; buds oily .... ***S. barrattiana*** (p. 54)

20b. Catkins with short, leafy stalks 21

21a. Leaves with indented net veins above, silky-hairy beneath .... ***S. vestita*** (see *S. barrattiana*, p. 54)

21b. Leaves flat above, short-hairy beneath 22

22a. Capsules with long (2–5 mm) stalks; catkins loosely flowered .... ***S. bebbiana*** (see *S. glauca*, p. 53)

22b. Capsules with short stalks; catkins compact 23

23a. Female catkins 1–2 cm long; leaf stalks 1–3 mm long, less than 3 times as long as buds .... ***S. brachycarpa*** (see *S. glauca,* p. 53)

23b. Female catkins, 2–5 cm long; leaf stalks 4–15 mm long, more than 3 times as long as buds ...... ***S. glauca*** (p. 53)

ARCTIC WILLOW
Salix arctica

General: Dwarf, deciduous shrub, usually less than 10 cm tall with trailing branches, often **forming mats**.

Leaves: Alternate, broadly oval, 2–6 cm long, sparsely hairy when mature, **glossy green above, pale with a greyish bloom beneath**; stalks 3–12 mm long; stipules small or absent.

Flowers: Tiny, in **dense, erect clusters (catkins) on leafy shoots,** either male or female on 1 shrub; seed (female) catkins **usually 2–4 cm long**; bracts brown to blackish; June to August, appear with the leaves.

Fruits: Silky, hairy capsules, 4–7 mm long; seeds tiny, tipped with a tuft of silky hairs, carried by wind.

Where Found: Moist to moderately dry, open sites; subalpine to alpine; Alaska to New Mexico.

Notes: Netted willow (***S. reticulata***, also known as ***S. saxi-montana*** and ***S. nivalis***) (lower photo) is another dwarf willow of moist slopes in the alpine zone from Alaska to New Mexico. It has dark, glossy, broadly elliptic to almost round leaves that are thick and leathery with a prominent network of veins. Its catkins are borne at the tips of the stems (not on small side branches), and its capsules are less than 3 mm long. • The young leaves, rhizomes and inner bark of arctic willow were occasionally eaten by native peoples. In some parts of the Arctic, this tiny shrub provides the only source of firewood. • The young leaves, stems and buds provide important browse for ptarmigan and other Arctic animals. • These dwarf shrubs live for decades by avoiding (rather than withstanding) cold temperatures, drying winds and abrasive, windblown ice crystals. They keep close to the ground and under the cover of snow in winter. • The fuzzy catkins are designed to trap the sun's rays. On calm, sunny days, female catkins can be up to 8.5° C warmer than the surrounding air, and male catkins can be as much as 7° C warmer than their surroundings. These warmer temperatures attract insect pollinators and speed the development of pollen and seeds in a short growing season.

BLUEBERRY WILLOW
Salix myrtillifolia

General: Low, deciduous shrub, usually 10–100 cm tall; branches greenish to reddish-brown, with short hairs when young, greyish and hairless with age, usually **spreading on ground and rooting**.

Leaves: Alternate, narrowly egg- to lance-shaped, usually widest above middle, **2–6 cm long, firm, hairless, green on both sides** (no whitish bloom on lower surface), **finely round-toothed**.

Flowers: Tiny, in **dense clusters (catkins) on short, leafy stalks**, either male or female on 1 shrub; pollen (male) catkins sweet scented, 1–2 cm long; seed (female) catkins **hairless, usually 2–3 cm long**; bracts light brown with dark tips; May to June, **with leaves**.

Fruits: Hairless, yellowish to brownish capsules, 3–6 mm long, with stalks about 1 mm long; seeds tiny, tipped with a tuft of silky hairs, carried by wind.

Where Found: Moist to wet, open or wooded sites; foothills to alpine; Alaska to Wyoming.

Notes: This species is also called ***S. novae-angliae***. • A few other willows also have hairless capsules and regularly toothed leaves that are green on both sides. **Variable willow** (***S. commutata***), also known as **undergreen willow**, is a low shrub (20–200 cm tall) with silky hairs on both sides of its leaves (especially when young). Its leaves are occasionally toothless or irregularly toothed, but they never have a greyish bloom. Variable willow forms thickets on moist slopes in the subalpine zone from the Yukon and NWT to Montana. • **Sandbar willow** (***S. exigua***, also called ***S. interior***) (lower photo), also known as **narrow-leaved willow**, is a taller shrub (50–400 cm) with 5–13 cm long, linear leaves that are about 10 times as long as wide. It grows on well-drained sites near water, often on floodplains, on plains, foothills and montane zones from Alaska to New Mexico.

FLAT-LEAVED WILLOW; PLANE-LEAVED WILLOW
Salix planifolia

General: Erect, deciduous shrub, 0.5–4 m tall; branches dark to **reddish-brown, shiny**, hairless, occasionally with a bluish-white bloom.

Leaves: Alternate, **elliptic, 3–5 cm long, essentially toothless and hairless** when mature, **shiny green** above, pale with a **whitish bloom beneath**; primary veins numerous and parallel.

Flowers: Tiny, in dense, **erect, stalkless clusters (catkins),** either male or female on 1 shrub; pollen (male) catkins 2–4 cm long; seed (female) catkins silky-hairy, **2–6 cm long**; bracts dark brown to black, silky-hairy; May to June, **before leaves**.

Fruits: Sparsely **silky-hairy capsules, 4–6 mm long (sometimes to 8 mm)**, with stalks less than 1 mm long; seeds tiny, tipped with a tuft of silky hairs, carried by wind.

Where Found: Moist, open or wooded sites, often near water; foothills to alpine; the Yukon and NWT to New Mexico.

Notes: This species is also called ***S. phylicifolia***. • Three common willows have hairless capsules, and also have hairless leaves with a whitish bloom on their lower surface. **Mountain willow** (***S. pseudomonticola***, also called ***S. monticola*** and ***S. padophylla***) (lower photo) has stalkless catkins and large (3–8 cm long), broad (1.5–3 cm wide) leaves with coarse, glandular teeth. It grows on moist slopes in foothills, montane and subalpine zones from the Yukon and NWT to New Mexico. Two species have catkins on short, leafy stalks. **Barclay's willow** (***S. barclayi***) has tawny or greenish capsules, and its glandular-toothed leaves usually have a few silky, white hairs when they are young. It grows in subalpine and alpine thickets from the Yukon and NWT to Montana. • **Farr's willow** (***S. farriae***) is often confused with Barclay's willow, but its leaves are hairless, even when young (except sometimes for a few fine hairs on the midrib), and are also usually toothless. It is a fairly low shrub (usually less than 1 m tall) found on moist to wet sites in subalpine and alpine zones from BC and Alberta to Wyoming.

SCOULER'S WILLOW
Salix scouleriana

General: Deciduous shrub, erect, 2–9 m tall, clumped, spindly; branches dark brown to yellowish-brown, densely **velvety to woolly, when young**.

Leaves: Alternate, lance- to egg-shaped, usually **broadest above middle**, 3–10 cm long**, wedge-shaped at base, rounded at tip**, essentially toothless, densely hairy when young, typically firm and dark green when mature with a whitish bloom and **short, stiff, rust-coloured hairs** lying flat on lower surface.

Flowers: Tiny, in **dense clusters (catkins)** that are stalkless or on short, leafy branchlets, either male or female on 1 shrub; pollen (male) catkins fluffy, pale yellow, 2–4 cm long; seed (female) catkins 2–4 cm long; bracts black to dark brown, silky; March to June, **before leaves**.

Fruits: Long-beaked, hairy capsules, 5–8 mm long, with short stalks and short stigmas; seeds tiny, tipped with a tuft of silky hairs, carried by wind.

Where Found: Moist to dry, open to wooded sites; foothills to montane; Alaska to New Mexico.

Notes: Little-tree willow (***S. arbusculoides***) (lower photo) is also a tall willow (1–7 m) with short, stiff hairs on the underside of its leaves. However, its leaves are regularly toothed and much more slender (narrowly elliptic to lance-shaped), and the hairs on its leaves are white and parallel. Its catkins appear with the leaves in late spring. Little-tree willow grows in moist, open or wooded sites in foothills, montane, subalpine and alpine zones from Alaska to BC and Alberta. • The bark was stripped and twisted to make twine and fishing nets that were strong when wet, but brittle when dry. • Willows are fast growing, producing large amounts of nutritious forage for many animals, including hares, porcupines, beavers, bears, deer and moose. The branches are often tall enough to stick out of the snow, providing important winter food for grouse and ptarmigan. The prolific male catkins offer a spring feast for bees.

GREY-LEAVED WILLOW
Salix glauca

General: Erect, deciduous shrub, 50–100 cm tall (sometimes to 2 m); branches dull, greyish to reddish-brown, usually hairy.

Leaves: Alternate, **elliptic to narrowly egg-shaped, 2–5 cm long** (sometimes to 10 cm), smooth and green above, **paler with a greyish bloom and usually slightly hairy beneath**; **stalks 4–15 mm long**, over 3 times as long as buds.

Flowers: Tiny, in **dense clusters (catkins) on leafy stalks**, either male or female on 1 shrub; pollen (male) catkins 1.5–2.5 cm long; **seed (female) catkins usually 2–5 cm long**; bracts yellowish to light brown, hairy; July to August, **with leaves**.

Fruits: Grey-hairy, green or yellowish **capsules 3–5 mm long** (sometimes to 8 mm), with stalks about 1 mm long; seeds tiny, tipped with a tuft of silky hairs, carried by wind.

Where Found: Moist, well-drained sites, often near streams; foothills to alpine; Alaska to New Mexico.

Notes: Short-fruited willow (***S. brachycarpa***) is very similar to grey-leaved willow, but its leaf stalks are shorter (1–3 mm long; less than 3 times as long as the bud), and its catkins are smaller (1–2 cm long). It grows in moist, open sites, often near water, in foothills, montane, subalpine and alpine zones from Alaska to Colorado. • **Bebb's willow** (***S. bebbiana***) (lower photo) is a common, tall (1–5 m) willow with sparsely hairy, long-stalked capsules in loose catkins on leafy branchlets. Its leaves are egg-shaped with some small, rounded teeth, and their lower surfaces have a whitish bloom and a raised network of veins, especially when young. Bebb's willow grows in wet to dry sites in foothills and montane zones from Alaska to New Mexico. • Willow bark contains salicin, a compound closely related to acetylsalicylic acid, the active ingredient in Aspirin. These chemicals were named for the genus *Salix*, since they were both originally derived from willow plants.

BARRATT'S WILLOW
Salix barrattiana

General: Low, deciduous shrub, with a balsam-like fragrance, usually 30–80 cm tall; branches dark, gnarled, hairy, somewhat **sticky and oily/resinous**; often form extensive thickets.

Leaves: Alternate, elliptic, widest above middle, usually 4–9 cm long, green and thinly **silky-hairy** above, pale and more densely hairy beneath.

Flowers: Tiny, in **stalkless, stiffly erect, dense clusters (catkins)**, either male or female on 1 shrub; pollen (male) catkins 2–5 cm long; **seed (female) catkins 4–11 cm long**; bracts blackish, long-hairy; June to July, with the leaves.

Fruits: Silky-hairy capsules, 5–6 mm long, nearly stalkless; seeds tiny, tipped with a tuft of silky hairs, carried by wind.

Where Found: Moist, open sites; subalpine to alpine; Alaska to Montana.

Notes: Several other willows have leaves with dense, white, silky hairs on their lower surfaces and often above as well. **Drummond's willow** (***S. drummondiana***) is a slightly taller shrub (1–2.5 m), distinguished by the pale greyish bloom on its hairless, yellowish twigs and the down-rolled edges of its leaves. It grows in moist sites in montane and subalpine zones from the southern Yukon to New Mexico. • The leaves of **Geyer's willow** (***S. geyeriana***) are densely silky on both sides when young, though they may become hairless with age. This tall (1.5–4.5 m) shrub also has a pale, waxy bloom on its twigs, but the bark is reddish, rather than yellowish. Its catkins are small (1–2.5 cm long) and loose, with thinly hairy capsules on relatively long stalks (1–2.5 mm). Geyer's willow grows on moist, open sites in foothills, montane and subalpine zones from southern BC and Montana to Colorado. • **Rock willow** (***S. vestita***) is a low shrub (less than 1 m tall) with crooked, angular, usually hairy branches. It has broad, leathery, distinctly veined leaves, with down-rolled, glandular edges. The fuzzy catkins develop late in the season after the leaves have fully expanded. Rock willow grows on moist slopes in subalpine to alpine zones from BC and Alberta to New Mexico.

HOARY WILLOW
Salix candida

General: Short, freely branched, deciduous shrub, 30–100 cm tall (sometimes to 1.5 m); branches brown, sparsely hairy, but white-woolly when young.

Leaves: Alternate**, narrowly elliptic to lance-shaped,** 3–10 cm long, 6–16 mm wide, **rolled under at edges, leathery**, dark green and sparsely hairy above, **densely white-woolly beneath**; stalks 3–9 mm long.

Flowers: Tiny, in **dense clusters (catkins) on short, leafy stalks**, either male or female on 1 shrub; pollen (male) about 1 cm long, with **reddish anthers**; seed (female) catkins 2–5 cm long; bracts brownish, hairy; May, with the leaves.

Fruits: Woolly capsules, 5–7 mm long, with red stigmas, red nectaries and 1 mm long stalks; seeds tiny, tipped with a tuft of silky hairs, carried by wind.

Where Found: Wet, open sites; foothills to montane; the Yukon and NWT to Colorado.

Notes: Felt-leaved willow (***S. alaxensis***) (lower photo), or **Alaska willow**, is a tall shrub or small tree 1–9 m tall. Like hoary willow, it has dense, woolly hairs on the lower side of its leaves, but its leaves are usually broader (2–2.5 cm wide). Its twigs are often permanently and conspicuously velvety-woolly with stalkless catkins that appear before the leaves. This willow grows on slopes in subalpine and alpine zones, often along streams, from Alaska to BC and Alberta. • Felt-leaved willow is a favourite food of moose, grouse and ptarmigan, especially during winter when other shrubs are buried by snow.

BOG BIRCH; DWARF BIRCH
Betula nana

General: Spreading to erect shrub, usually **1–2 m tall** (ranging from 0.1–6 m); young branches hairy and covered with **wart-like, crystalline resin glands** (like tiny octopus suckers).

Leaves: Alternate, **round** (sometimes broadly egg-shaped), usually **1–2 cm long**, with 2–3 veins and 6–10 rounded teeth per side, glandular, somewhat **leathery**, scarlet to reddish-brown in autumn.

Flowers: Tiny, in dense clusters (catkins), male or female, with both sexes on same branch; pollen (male) catkins 1–2 cm long, slender, hanging; **seed (female) catkins 1–1.5 cm long, 3–5 mm thick, erect**; May to July.

Fruits: Round, flattened, **narrowly winged nutlets**, 2 mm wide, hidden by scales of erect catkins.

Where Found: Dry to (more commonly) wet, open sites; foothills to alpine; Alaska to Colorado.

Notes: This species is also known as ***B. glandulosa***. • **Swamp birch** (***B. pumila***, also called ***B. glandulifera***), also called **scrub birch**, is very similar to bog birch, and many taxonomists include these 2 shrubs in the same species. Swamp birch has egg-shaped leaves with 4 or more veins and 10 or more teeth per side, twigs that are less densely glandular than those of bog birch, and nutlets that have broad wings (each as wide as the body of the nutlet). It grows in wet sites in the foothills and montane zones from the southern Yukon and NWT to Wyoming. • It is easy to stumble over bog birch when you are hiking in summer, which is why some people call this shrub 'shin-trippers' or 'shin-tangle.' The branches spread out and sag under the weight of the snow, often leaving only their tips exposed to the cold, dry winter air.

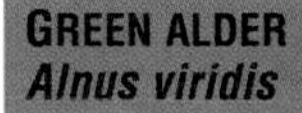

GREEN ALDER
Alnus viridis

General: Clumped, deciduous shrub, 1–4 m tall; branches essentially hairless (finely glandular when young), reddish-brown to greyish-black.

Leaves: Alternate, oval, 4–8 cm long, **pointed**, dark yellowish-green, **often shiny, edged with fine, sharp, single or double teeth**.

Flowers: Tiny, in dense clusters (catkins), male or female, with both sexes growing on same twig; pollen (male) catkins 3–8 cm long, slender, loosely hanging; **seed (female) catkins woody, egg-shaped**, 1–1.5 cm long, in clusters of 3–6 on new twigs; May to July, at same time as leaves.

Fruits: Broad-winged nutlets, 2 mm long, shed from **cone-like** catkins.

Where Found: Along streams and in moist woods; foothills to subalpine; Alaska to Colorado.

Notes: This species is also known as ***A. crispa*** and ***A. sinuata***. • **Mountain alder** (***A. incana***, also called ***A. rugosa*** and ***A. tenuifolia***) (lower photo) is distinguished from green alder by its dull green, wavy-lobed, double-toothed leaves. Its seed cones grow before the leaves appear in spring on twigs from the previous year. Mountain alder grows on riverbanks and lakeshores in foothills, montane and subalpine zones from Alaska to New Mexico. • Some native peoples treated hemorrhoids with alder bark tea. Green alder was mainly used as fuel for smoking fish, meat and hides. A red dye intended for hides and fishnets was made from the twigs and inner bark—thought to make the nets harder for fish to see. • Beavers feed on these shrubs, and use them to construct lodges and dams. • Alders are an important colonizing species, because their roots contain nitrogen-fixing bacteria. They can grow rapidly in nitrogen-poor soils, and they increase local nitrogen levels with their decaying leaves and branches. Their tiny flowers are wind pollinated.

Key to Gooseberries & Currants (*Ribes* Species)

1a. Stems more or less spiny and usually bristly (gooseberries) 2

2a. Flowers saucer-shaped, 4–15 in spreading or hanging clusters; flower stalks jointed near the top just below the ovary (or berry) 3

3a. Leaves abundantly hairy and glandular; berries red .... ***R. montigenum***
.... (see *R. lacustre*, p. 57)

3b. Leaves hairless (or nearly so), not glandular; berries dark purple to black .... ***R. lacustre*** (p. 57)

2b. Flowers bell-shaped, 1–3 from leaf axils; flower stalks not jointed near top 4

4a. Older stems with grey, flaky bark, deep red underneath, with few spines; stamens at least twice as long as petals .... ***R. inerme***
.... (see *R. oxyacanthoides*, p. 57)

4b. Older stems whitish-grey, spiny; stamens about as long as petals
.... ***R. oxyacanthoides*** (p. 57)

1b. Stems not spiny or bristly (currants) 5

5a. Leaf lobes conspicuously rounded 6

6a. Flowers bright yellow, hairless .... ***R. aureum***
.... (see *R. hudsonianum*, p. 58)

6b. Flowers white, glandular-hairy 7

7a. Berries bluish to black; flower tube about as long as sepals; leaves 4–7 cm wide .... ***R. viscosissimum***
.... (see *R. cereum*, p. 58)

7b. Berries red; flower tube twice as long as sepals; leaves 1–4 cm broad .... ***R. cereum*** (p. 58)

5b. Leaf lobes not conspicuously rounded, more or less sharply pointed 8

8a. Leaves sprinkled with yellow crystalline glands ('resin dots') on lower surface 8

9a. Ovaries and berries with resin dots; flowers white, in erect clusters ..... ***R. hudsonianum*** (p. 58)

9b. Ovaries and berries without resin dots; flowers greenish to yellow, in nodding clusters
.... ***R. americanum***
.... (see *R. hudsonianum*, p. 58)

8b. Leaves without resin dots 10

10a. Flowers greenish-white to purplish; berries dark red; sepals hairless on outside, 2–2.5 mm long .... ***R. glandulosum***
.... (see *R. lacustre*, p. 57)

10b. Flowers red to purplish; berries bluish-black; sepals hairy on outside, 3–4 mm long .... ***R. laxiflorum***
.... (see *R. lacustre*, p. 57)

NORTHERN GOOSEBERRY
Ribes oxyacanthoides

General: Erect to sprawling, deciduous shrub, 30–90 cm tall; bristly branches, often with **1–3 spines up to 1 cm long at nodes**, yellowish, pale grey with age.

Leaves: Alternate, somewhat maple-leaf–like, with 3–5 lobes, **squared or slightly heart-shaped at base, 2–4 cm wide**, irregularly round-toothed, usually glandular-hairy beneath.

Flowers: Whitish to pale greenish-yellow, about 8 mm long, tubular, with 5 small, erect petals and 5 l**arger, spreading sepals, 1–2 from leaf axils**; stamens short, reaching past petal tips; May to June.

Fruits: Smooth, reddish to **bluish-purple berries**, 10–12 mm across.

Where Found: Moist woods; plains to montane; the Yukon and NWT to Wyoming.

Notes: This species has also been called ***R. hirtellum*** and ***R. setosum***. • **White-stemmed gooseberry** (***R. inerme***) is distinguished by its white, relatively spine-free older branches and its long stamens, which project out well past the petals. It grows in foothills and montane forests from BC and Alberta to New Mexico. • Northern gooseberries are often eaten fresh, and they make excellent jams and pies. • Gooseberry thorns were often used as needles for probing boils, removing splinters, and tattooing. • In the early 1900s, 10 million pine seedlings infected with blister rust (*Cronartium ribicola*) were brought to North America from Europe, and the rust soon spread to infect the native, 5-needled pines. To reproduce, rust must spend part of its life cycle on an alternate host. *Ribes* species are the alternate host for blister rust, so a program to eradicate these shrubs was unsuccessfully attempted.

BRISTLY BLACK CURRANT; BLACK GOOSEBERRY
Ribes lacustre

General: Deciduous shrub, erect to spreading, 0.5–1.5 m tall; branches **with small prickles and with larger thorns at leaf and branch bases**, cinnamon-coloured when mature.

Leaves: Alternate, **maple-leaf–like** with 3–5 deeply cut, palmate lobes, heart-shaped at base, about 3–4 cm across, coarsely toothed, essentially hairless.

Flowers: Reddish to maroon, **saucer-shaped**, about 6 mm across, glandular hairs on ovary and stalk, in **hanging elongated flower clusters** (racemes) of 7–15; May to August.

Fruits: Dark purple to black berries, 5–8 mm across, **bristly** with glandular hairs.

Where Found: Moist, wooded or open sites; foothills to alpine; the Yukon and NWT to Colorado and Utah.

Notes: Mountain gooseberry (***R. montigenum***), also called **mountain prickly currant**, is very similar to prickly black currant, but its leaves are glandular-hairy on both sides, and its berries are bright red. It grows on rocky sites in montane to alpine zones from southern BC to New Mexico. • Some currants with bristly fruits do not have bristles or thorns on their branches. **Skunk currant** (***R. glandulosum***) has red berries, small (2–2.5 mm long), hairless sepals and greenish-white to pale pink flowers. It grows in moist sites in foothills and montane zones in the Yukon and NWT to BC and Alberta. • **Trailing black currant** (***R. laxiflorum***) has bluish-black berries, larger (3–4 mm long), hairy sepals and red to purplish flowers. It grows in moist, subalpine woods in the Yukon, BC, Alberta and Idaho. • Bristly black currants are edible, but insipid. • The spines of bristly black currant can cause a serious **allergic** reaction in some people. Some native peoples considered the branches (and by extension, the fruit) poisonous. However, this shrub could be used to advantage; the branches were thought to ward off evil forces.

R. laxiflorum

NORTHERN BLACK CURRANT
Ribes hudsonianum

General: Erect to ascending, deciduous shrub with a **sweet, 'tomcat' odour**, 50–150 cm tall; branches smooth (**no prickles**), with yellow, crystalline resin dots.

Leaves: Alternate, **maple-leaf–like** with 3–5 lobes, usually **5–7 cm wide**, sharply toothed, dotted with yellow **resins glands** beneath.

Flowers: White, about 5 mm across, broadly funnel-shaped, with 5 spreading lobes, **6–12 in erect to spreading clusters** (racemes); May to July.

Fruits: Black berries with a whitish, waxy bloom, usually speckled with a few yellow **resin dots**, 5–10 mm wide.

Where Found: Moist to wet, shady sites; foothills to montane; Alaska to Wyoming.

Notes: Wild black currant (*R. americanum*) also has black berries and leaves with resin dots on their lower surface. However, its ovaries and berries have no resin dots, and its greenish to yellowish, more tubular flowers form showy, nodding clusters. Wild black currant grows in moist woods on the plains and foothills from Alberta to New Mexico. • **Golden currant (*R. aureum*)** has showy, fragrant clusters of large (6–9 mm long), bright yellow to reddish flowers. It grows in well-drained sites, often along streams, on plains and foothills from Alberta to New Mexico. • These berries were occasionally used by native peoples, but they were not widely used for food. They can be used to make black currant jelly or jam, which is delicious with meat, fish or bannock. According to Hearne (1802), large quantities of northern black currants can be strongly **purgative**, and can even cause **vomiting** at the same time but not if they are mixed with cranberries. • The Thompson tribe believed that this shrub had a calming effect on children, so sprigs of it were often put in baby carriers.

SQUAW CURRANT; WAX CURRANT
Ribes cereum

General: Deciduous shrub, erect to spreading, 0.5–1.5 m tall; branches numerous, without thorns, finely glandular-hairy when young, greyish to red-brown when mature.

Leaves: Alternate, **kidney-shaped to broadly fan-shaped, 1–4 cm wide**, coarsely round-toothed, usually with **3–5 shallow, palmate lobes**, nearly hairless to sticky, glandular-hairy.

Flowers: White, tinged greenish or pinkish, **tubular**, with 5 tiny, erect petals and 5 small, spreading sepals, about 6–8 mm long, usually **sticky glandular-hairy**, hanging in small clusters (short racemes) of 1–8; May to July.

Fruits: Red berries (**currants**), 6–7 mm across.

Where Found: Dry slopes; plains to montane; BC to New Mexico.

Notes: Sticky currant (*R. viscosissimum*) is similar to squaw currant, but its leaves are larger (4–7 cm wide) and more deeply lobed, and its berries are black and about 1 cm across. Sticky currant grows in open, moist to dry forests of the foothills and montane zones from southern BC and Alberta to Colorado. • These sticky, aromatic fruits are generally tasteless to bitter, so they are not very good either raw or in jellies. Native peoples used them fresh or dried, but they also warned that consuming **too many could cause illness**. Although the berries are eaten only occasionally, these shrubs are very common, and they could provide food in an emergency. Some tribes considered them a tonic, and ate them to relieve diarrhea. • The flowers provide an important source of nectar for hummingbirds early in the year. • The species name *cereum* means 'waxy,' in reference to the waxy appearance of the glandular leaves.

R. viscosissimum

ROCKY MOUNTAIN MAPLE; DOUGLAS MAPLE
Acer glabrum var. douglasii

General: Deciduous shrub or small tree, 1–7 m tall (sometimes up to 10 m), clumped; branches **opposite**, with greyish bark and reddish twigs.

Leaves: Opposite, broadly heart-shaped, with 3–5 palmate lobes (**typical maple-leaf**), coarsely sharp-toothed, **2–10 cm across**; dark green above, lighter below, bright yellow-orange to **crimson in autumn**.

Flowers: Yellowish-green, about 8 mm across, with 5 petals and 5 sepals, usually male or female (with sexes on separate shrubs); hanging in loose, fragrant clusters (cymes) of 5–15; April to June.

Fruits: V-shaped pairs of wrinkled, winged seeds (keys) hanging on slender stalks, greenish to tan, tinged red when young; seeds about 5 mm across; wings about 2 cm long.

Where Found: Moist, sheltered sites; foothills to montane; central BC and Alberta to New Mexico.

Notes: This shrub has also been called ***A. douglasii***. • **Canyon maple** (***A. grandidentatum***), also known as **wasatch maple**, also has typical 'maple' leaves, but its leaf edges have wide hollows and blunt teeth, and its flowers and keys are borne in even-stalked, umbrella-like clusters. Canyon maple grows in dry sites from Idaho and Montana to New Mexico. • **Manitoba maple** (***A. negundo***), also known as **box-elder**, may not be recognized as a maple, because its leaves are pinnately compound with 3–5 lance-shaped leaflets (resembling ash leaves). It is widespread across North America, and in many areas it has escaped from cultivation. In the Rockies it grows naturally along streams from Idaho to New Mexico. • Large tracts of land in the foothills of the southern Rockies are often covered by oak brush. Oaks (*Quercus* spp.) can be very difficult to identify, and 2 'species' are often found on the same bush. **Gambel's oak** (***Quercus gambelii***) is the most common species. It is a 3–5 m tall shrub with deeply lobed, 5–10 cm long leaves and 12–15 mm long acorns (the cap covers 1/3 or more of the nut). It grows on dry slopes in the foothills from southern Wyoming to New Mexico.

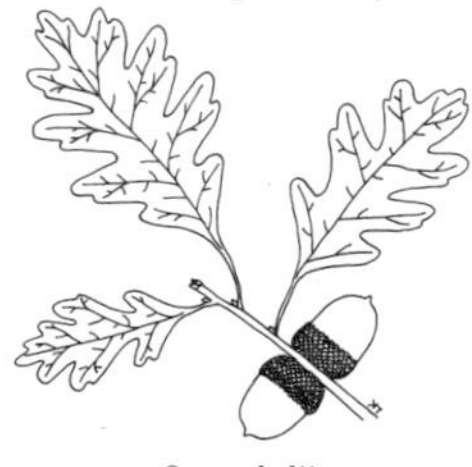
Q. gambelii

DEVIL'S CLUB
Oplopanax horridus

General: Strong-smelling, **spiny, coarse**, deciduous shrub, **1–3 m tall**; stems erect to sprawling, thick, armed with many long spines, crooked, seldom branched, often entangled.

Leaves: Alternate, **broadly maple-leaf–like** with 5–7 toothed lobes, **10–40 cm wide, prickly ribs** beneath, spreading on long, bristly stalks near stem tips.

Flowers: Greenish-white, 5–6 mm long, with 5 petals and sepals, nearly stalkless, in dense heads (umbels) forming **10–25 cm long, pyramid-shaped clusters** (panicles) at stem tips; May to July.

Fruits: Bright red, slightly flattened, berry-like drupes, 4–6 mm long, in **showy clusters**.

Where Found: Moist to wet, shady sites; foothills to montane; BC and Alberta to Idaho and Montana.

Notes: These berries are not edible. The young, fleshy stems can be eaten, but some people have an **allergic reaction** to the spines. The spines break off easily and can cause infections when they remain embedded in the skin. • The wood has a distinctive, sweet smell. The aromatic roots were mixed with tobacco and smoked to relieve headaches • The stems have been used medicinally. Dried pieces, scraped free of prickles, were steeped in boiling water to make medicinal teas and were taken, in small quantities before meals, to treat flu and other illnesses. Devil's club tea was also said to improve appetite and help people to gain weight, but the patient could gain too much weight if it was taken for too long.

HIGHBUSH CRANBERRY; SQUASHBERRY
Viburnum edule

General: Erect or straggly, deciduous shrub, 50–200 cm tall; branches smooth, reddish to dark grey.

Leaves: Opposite, 3–10 cm long and wide, maple-leaf–like, with 3 shallow lobes, sharply toothed, hairy beneath.

Flowers: White, 4–7 mm across, broadly funnel-shaped with 5 spreading lobes, 3–30 in **rounded to flat-topped clusters (umbels) 1–3 cm across**, above a single pair of leaves; May to July.

Fruits: Red to orange, berry-like drupes, about 1 cm long, juicy, with a single flat stone, strong-smelling.

Where Found: Moist, shady sites; foothills to subalpine; Alaska to Colorado.

Notes: Pembina (***V. opulus***) (lower photo), also called **American-bush cranberry**, is a larger shrub (1–4 m tall) with a ring of large (12–25 mm wide), showy, sterile flowers around the outer edge of each flower cluster. Its leaves have deeper, more slender, pointed lobes than those of highbush cranberry. It grows in moist woods in foothills and montane zones from southern BC and Alberta to Wyoming. • In some areas, 'highbush cranberry' refers to *V. opulus* and *V. edule* is called 'lowbush cranberry'; in still others, 'lowbush cranberry' refers to lingonberry (p. 79)—a good example of why common names can be very confusing. • The berries of both of these shrubs are an excellent source of vitamin C. They are picked in autumn and boiled to make juice, wine or jelly. Some compare the smell to dirty socks, but the flavour is good. Raw fruits are very sour and acidic; large quantities can cause **vomiting** and **cramps**.

BLACK ELDERBERRY
Sambucus racemosa

General: Erect, deciduous shrub, 1–3 m tall, often clumped, **strong-smelling; branches opposite**, dark reddish-brown, often sprouting from base; **twigs soft, pithy**, often whitish.

Leaves: Opposite, pinnately compound with **5–7 lance-shaped leaflets, sharply toothed**, often with hairs beneath; leaflets 5–15 cm long, **slender pointed**.

Flowers: White, 3–6 mm across, in crowded, round to **pyramidal clusters** (cymes), with a strong, unpleasant smell; April to June.

Fruits: Bright red or purplish-black, berry-like drupes, 5–6 mm across, with 3–5 smooth seeds, in dense clusters 4–10 cm long.

Where Found: Moist sites; foothills to subalpine; BC and Alberta to New Mexico.

Notes: This species includes 2 varieties that are distinguished by their fruit colour: var. *melanocarpa* (previously known as ***S. melanocarpa***), which has purplish-black fruit, and var. *leucocarpa* (previously known as ***S. pubens***), which has red fruit. • **Blue elderberry** (***S. cerulea***, also known as ***S. glauca***) usually has 9 leaflets (though it can have 5 or 7), its flowers form flat-topped clusters, and its fruits are blue with a whitish bloom. It grows along streams and on rocky slopes in foothills and montane zones from BC and Alberta to New Mexico. • The berries are unpalatable, and they can cause **nausea** if they are eaten raw, but ripe berries are edible when cooked. Although they are small and seedy, they have been eaten by native peoples for 1,000s of years. Today, the berries are used to make jam, jelly, pies and wine, and the flowers can be used to make tea. • The stems, bark, leaves and roots contain **cyanide-producing glycosides**, and therefore they are **poisonous**, especially when fresh. Tea made from the bark and leaves was used by some tribes as an emetic and purgative. The pithy branches can be hollowed out to fashion whistles, drinking straws, blowguns and pipe-stems, but remember, they are **toxic**.

COMMON SNOWBERRY
Symphoricarpos albus

General: Deciduous shrub, erect, usually **50–75 cm** tall (can reach 2 m); branches **opposite, slender**, hairless; often forms colonies from rhizomes.

Leaves: Opposite, elliptic to oval, usually **2–4 cm long, thin, pale green**; edges smooth to slightly wavy-lobed.

Flowers: Pink to white and broadly funnel-shaped, 4–7 mm long, hairy inside; **stamens and style do not protrude** from flower; styles hairless; anthers 1–1.5 mm long; in small clusters (racemes) at or near branch tips; June to August.

Fruits: White, waxy, berry-like drupes 6–10 mm across, in small clusters, persist through winter.

Where Found: Well-drained, open or wooded sites; plains to lower subalpine; BC and Alberta to Colorado.

Notes: Western snowberry (*S. occidentalis*), also called **wolfberry**, is very similar to common snowberry, but it has hairy styles and large (1.5–2 mm) anthers, both of which project from its flowers. It grows on open sites in the foothills and lower montane zones from BC and Alberta to New Mexico. • **Mountain snowberry** (*S. oreophilus*) has longer (7–12 mm), more tubular flowers. It grows on dry, open sites in the foothills and montane zones, from southern BC to New Mexico. • These bitter berries are **toxic** when eaten in quantity. The branches, leaves and roots are also **poisonous**, causing **vomiting** and diarrhea. • Some native peoples called snowberries 'corpse berries' or 'snake's berries.' Because of their white colour, they were believed to be the ghosts of saskatoon berries and part of the spirit world, not to be eaten by the living.

BRACTED HONEYSUCKLE; BLACK TWINBERRY
Lonicera involucrata

General: Deciduous shrub, erect to spreading, usually 1–2 m tall (sometimes up to 3 m); **twigs greenish, 4-sided**.

Leaves: Opposite, elliptic to broadly lance-shaped, 5–15 cm long, **pointed, often broadest above middle**, hairy, gland-dotted beneath.

Flowers: Pale yellow, tubular, 1–2 cm long, with **large (1–1.5 cm long), broad, green to red or purple bracts** at base, in opposite pairs from leaf axils; May to July.

Fruits: Shiny **pairs of purple-black berries**, about 8 mm across, with pairs of broad, **red to purplish bracts** at base; bracts **spreading or bent backwards**, often shiny.

Where Found: Moist to wet, open or wooded sites; foothills to subalpine; BC and Alberta to New Mexico.

Notes: Utah honeysuckle (*L. utahensis*) (bottom photo), also called **red twinberry**, has similar flowers, but its flower bracts are small and inconspicuous. It produces pairs of red berries that are fused together at their bases. Its leaves are usually small (2–8 cm long), with blunt or broadly rounded tips. Utah honeysuckle grows in moist, wooded or open sites in foothills and montane zones from southern BC and Alberta to Utah and Wyoming. • Bracted honeysuckle berries are inedible. They **may be somewhat poisonous**, but they are so disgusting there is little chance of anyone eating enough to worry. However, the berries of Utah honeysuckle are juicy and edible—a good emergency water source. • Birds, bears and other animals eat these berries in large quantities. • The species name *involucrata* means 'with an involucre,' referring to the showy bracts at the base of each flower and fruit.

TWINING HONEYSUCKLE
Lonicera dioica

General: Twining, woody vine, up to 6 m long; branches smooth, green or purplish when young, becoming brown or grey with shredding bark.

Leaves: Opposite, egg-shaped to oblong, blunt-tipped or round-tipped, **5–8 cm long**, dark green and hairless above, paler and usually hairy beneath, essentially **stalkless**; 1–4 **uppermost pairs, joined at bases,** encircle the stem.

Flowers: Yellow or orange, often purplish or reddish with age, **15–25 mm long, narrow and funnel-shaped** with a bump on 1 side near base, **2-lipped**, with 5 long, spreading lobes, stalkless, in **whorled clusters, from centres of cupped pairs of upper leaves**; June to July.

Fruits: Red berries, 8–12 mm long, in dense clusters at stem tips in leaf cups.

Where Found: Dry, shaded sites; foothills to montane; the southern Yukon and NWT to southern BC and Alberta.

Notes: Western trumpet honeysuckle (*L. ciliosa*), also called **orange honeysuckle**, is very similar to twining honeysuckle, but it has larger (2.5–4 cm long), orange-yellow to orange-red flowers that are only slightly 2-lipped and that end in much smaller lobes. Its leaves are hairless, except for a fringe along their edges. It grows in shady foothills and montane zones from southern BC and Montana to New Mexico. • These vines can climb up to 6 m high on the branches of small trees. Their long, orange, scentless flowers are adapted to pollination by hummingbirds. • **Nausea and vomiting** have been reported by people who have eaten honeysuckle. • Because honeysuckle branches are hollow between the nodes, they were used as stems for corn-cob pipes and toy (rose-hip) pipes.

SHRUBBY PENSTEMON
Penstemon fruticosus

General: Low, bushy shrub, or semi-shrub, 5–40 cm tall; stems freely branched, often reddish and brittle, glandular-hairy near top, forming **dense clumps from a woody base**.

Leaves: Opposite and in basal clusters, linear to **lance-shaped**, 2–6 cm long, **dark green and hairless above**, saw-toothed to nearly toothless.

Flowers: Bluish-lavender to pale purple, 3–5 cm long, tubular, 2-lipped, long white-hairy on lower lip, **in pairs in short clusters** (racemes) at branch tips; calyx densely glandular-hairy; anthers long-woolly; July to August.

Fruits: Capsules, 8–12 mm long.

Where Found: Dry, rocky sites; montane to alpine; southern BC and Alberta to Wyoming.

Notes: Elliptic-leaved penstemon (*P. ellipticus*) (lower photo) is a low (5–15 cm tall), mat-forming, semi-woody species with broader leaves (elliptic to egg-shaped). It grows on rocky slopes in montane, subalpine and alpine zones from southern BC and Alberta to Idaho and Montana. • Not all *Penstemons* are woody; several species are described in the Herbs section (pp. 195–96). • The leaves and flowers of shrubby penstemon were added to cooking pits to flavour wild onions (p. 91) and the roots of arrow-leaved balsamroot (p. 238). • Bees and hummingbirds pollinate these long, tubular flowers. • The genus name *Penstemon* was derived from the Latin *pente*, 'five,' and *stemon*, 'thread,' referring to the 5 (4 fertile, plus 1 sterile) stamens of these flowers. Penstemons are sometimes called 'beard-tongues,' either because of their hairy lower lips, or because of their bearded, sterile stamen.

MALLOW NINEBARK
Physocarpus malvaceus

General: Deciduous shrub, 50–200 cm tall, with **star-shaped hairs**; arching branches, with **brown, shredding bark**.

Leaves: Alternate, **somewhat maple-leaf–like**, with 3–5 lobes, about **2–6 cm long** and wide, toothed, **strongly veined, shiny and dark green above**, paler beneath.

Flowers: White, saucer-shaped, about 1 cm across, with several 5-rounded petals, in rounded clusters (corymbs) at branch tips; June to July.

Fruits: Reddish, **egg-shaped pairs of flattened, keeled pods** (follicles) with erect styles, joined on lower 1/2, **fuzzy**, about 5 mm long.

Where Found: Dry, open or lightly wooded slopes; montane; southern BC and Alberta to Wyoming.

Notes: Rocky Mountain ninebark (***P. monogynus***) is a smaller (usually less than 1 m tall) shrub with 1–3 cm long leaves, 6 mm wide flowers and 3–4 mm long pods. Its pods are also swollen and rounded (not keeled), and their styles spread outwards from the centre. Rocky Mountain ninebark grows on dry, open or wooded slopes in foothills and montane zones from Wyoming to New Mexico. In autumn, its leaves turn many slopes orange and red. • The Okanagan used mallow ninebark as a 'good-luck' charm to protect their hunting equipment. • Mallow ninebark makes an attractive garden addition—best grown from cuttings. Seeds should be sown in autumn, but they are slow to become established. • The common name 'ninebark' was given to these shrubs because they were believed to have 9 layers of shredding bark. The genus name *Physocarpus* was taken from the Greek *physa*, 'bladder,' and *carpos*, fruit,' because of the inflated pods of most species.

BLACK HAWTHORN
Crataegus douglasii

General: Deciduous shrub or small tree, 1–4 m tall (sometimes to 8 m); rough and scaly, grey branches, with **straight thorns 1–2 cm long**.

Leaves: Alternate, about **3–6 cm long and almost as wide**, egg-shaped, **sharply toothed**, often **lobed at tip**, wedge-shaped at base, leathery, glossy and dark green above, **hairless** beneath; stalks with scattered glands.

Flowers: Whitish, saucer-shaped, about 1–1.5 cm wide, with 5 round petals, in showy, flat-topped clusters (corymbs), unpleasantly scented; May to June.

Fruits: Blackish-purple pomes (like tiny apples) about 1 cm long, pulpy, withered before winter, containing 1 large nutlet.

Where Found: Well-drained sites, but often near water; foothills to subalpine; BC and Alberta to Wyoming.

Notes: River hawthorn (***C. rivularis***) is very similar to black hawthorn; some taxonomists classify these 2 shrubs as varieties of the same species. River hawthorn generally has longer thorns (2–3 cm), narrower (1.5–2 times as long as wide), toothed, but not lobed leaves and leaf stalks without glands. It grows on well-drained slopes in valleys and along streams in the foothills, from Idaho and Wyoming to New Mexico. • **Red hawthorn** (***C. columbiana***, also called ***C. chrysocarpa*** and ***C. rotundifolia***) has red or reddish-purple pomes and longer thorns (4–7 cm), with leaves that are hairy on both sides. It grows on well-drained, open slopes, often near streams, on plains and foothills from southern BC and Alberta to Idaho and Montana. • This genus is easily identified, even in winter, by the long, simple thorns on its branches, but as a group, it is perhaps the most difficult to classify of the rose family. Hundreds of names have been proposed for the many 'species' of hawthorn. • The fruits or 'haws' are edible, but they are not very juicy. • Eye scratches from these thorns can result in **blindness**.

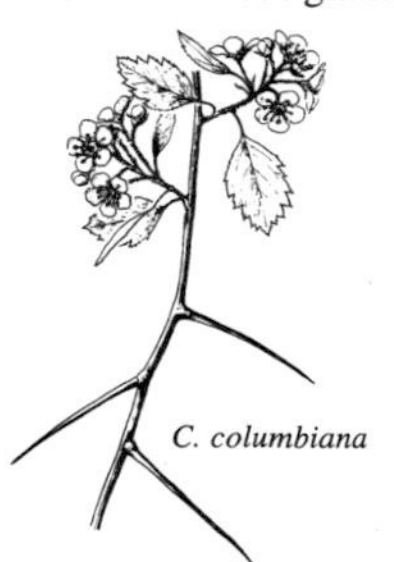

C. columbiana

BIRCH-LEAVED SPIRAEA
Spiraea betulifolia

General: Deciduous shrub, usually 40–70 cm tall, spreading from rhizomes.

Leaves: Alternate, oval, 2–7 cm long, often widest above middle, **irregularly coarse-toothed towards tip**.

Flowers: White, often tinged pink to purple, saucer-shaped, about 5 mm across, with 5 tiny petals and 25–50 long stamens, in **flat-topped clusters (corymbs), 3–8 cm across**; May to July.

Fruits: Beaked, pod-like capsules (follicles), 3 mm long, in clusters of 5 per flower, joined at base.

Where Found: Moist to dry, open or wooded sites; foothills to subalpine; BC and Alberta to Wyoming.

Notes: This species has also been called ***S. lucida***. • Birch-leaved spiraea leaves could be confused with those of saskatoon (p. 66), but that shrub has broader, more regularly toothed leaves with heart-shaped bases. • **Subalpine spiraea** (***S. splendens***, also known as ***S. densiflora***) also has flat-topped clusters of flowers, but its flowers are deep pink, and its stems are usually decumbent, seldom reaching over 40 cm in height. It grows in moist sites from BC and Alberta to Wyoming. • Wild spireas are attractive plants that could be used in gardens. These hardy shrubs are easily grown from cuttings, offshoots or seeds, but once they are established, they tend to spread rapidly by rhizomes, and they can be difficult to control. • Blue grouse eat the young leaves, and deer browse on the shrubs. • The common name 'birch-leaved spiraea' and the species name *betulifolia* (from the Latin *betula*, 'birch,' and *folium*, 'leaf') both refer to the similarity between the leaves of this shrub and those of swamp birch (p. 55).

S. splendens

MOUNTAIN MAHOGANY
Cercocarpus montanus

General: Deciduous shrub, 1–2 m tall (rarely to 3 m); branches smooth, grey or brown.

Leaves: Alternate, lance-shaped to rounded, **wedge-shaped at base**, 1–5 cm long, **with shallow, round teeth** and **prominent veins**, dark green above, paler beneath, **short-stalked**.

Flowers: Greenish, bell-shaped, hairy, 6–7 mm wide, 3–6 mm long (8–14 mm in fruit), with 5 backward-bent sepals, no petals, 25–40 stamens, and 1 pistil with a **feathery style, 1–3 in leaf axils** on short side shoots; April to July

Fruits: Hairy, dry, seed-like, about 1 cm long with a **feathery tail** (style) 3–6 cm long.

Where Found: Dry, open or lightly wooded slopes; plains to montane; Montana to New Mexico.

Notes: Mountain mahogany wood was used to make weaving combs and handles for tools. • To dye wool and buckskins brown and baskets red, the Navajo boiled the root bark and then soaked and rubbed the material in this decoction. Sometimes other plants were used to produce different colours: the ashes of dried yucca leaves (p. 95) for a lighter brown or tan, ashes of juniper needles (pp. 47–48) for a darker brown and mountain alder bark (p. 55) for a reddish-brown. Young plants or the leaves of old plants were powdered and mixed with salt and water for use as a laxative. • For good luck, hunters sometimes chewed the leaves from shrubs that had been browsed by deer. • The genus name *Cercocarpus* was taken from the Greek *kerkos*, 'tail,' and *carpos*, 'fruit,' in reference to the long, feathery, persistent tails (styles) on the fruits of these shrubs. The species name *montanus* means 'of the mountains.'

CHOKE CHERRY
Prunus virginiana

General: Deciduous shrub or small tree, erect to straggling, 1–5 m tall; branches often twisted, smooth, reddish-grey to greyish-brown, with **small, raised, horizontal slits** (pores called lenticels).

Leaves: Alternate, oval, **often widest above middle**, 3–10 cm long, pointed at tip, rounded at base, with **fine, sharp teeth** on edges, hairless on upper surface; stalks with **2–3 prominent, reddish glands near base** of blade.

Flowers: Creamy **white**, saucer-shaped, 10–12 mm across, with 5 broad petals, in erect, **bottlebrush-like clusters** (racemes) 5–15 cm long at branch tips; May to June.

Fruits: Shiny, **dark red to black cherries** (drupes) **6–8 mm across**, in hanging clusters.

Where Found: Dry to moist, open sites; plains to montane; southern NWT to New Mexico.

Notes: This species is also known as ***P. melanocarpa***. • Most other wild cherries in the Rockies have flowers and fruits in flat-topped clusters (umbels or corymbs). • **Bitter cherry** (***P. emarginata***) has larger (8–12 mm long), red to black cherries, and its leaves are usually rounded or blunt-tipped with rounded teeth. It grows mainly west of the continental divide in the foothills from BC to Utah. • All parts of the choke cherry (except the flesh of the fruit) contain the **poison** hydrocyanic acid. There are reports of children dying after eating large amounts of choke cherries without removing the stones, but native peoples have been eating this fruit, pits and all, for centuries with no reported cases of poisoning. • Choke cherries were among the most important berries for many tribes. They were collected after the 1st frost, which makes them sweeter, and were eaten dried or cooked, often as an addition to pemmican or stews. Large quantities were collected, pulverized with rocks, formed into patties (about 15 cm in diameter and 2 cm thick), and dried for winter use. Today, choke cherries are used to make jelly, syrup, sauce and wine. Bitter cherry can be used in the same way. • The astringent cherries can cause a puckering or choking sensation when they are eaten, hence the name 'choke cherry.'

PIN CHERRY
Prunus pensylvanica

General: Deciduous shrub or small tree, 1–5 m tall; branches **glossy reddish-brown**, with prominent, raised, horizontal slits (pores called **lenticels**).

Leaves: Alternate, **oval to lance-shaped**, 3–10 cm long, tapered to a **long point at tip, rounded at base**, with **fine, rounded teeth** on edges, stalks with **2 small, dark glands** near base of blade.

Flowers: White, saucer-shaped, 6–12 mm across, with 5 broad petals, in **flat-topped clusters** (umbels) of 3–6 along branches; May to June.

Fruits: Shiny, **bright red cherries** (drupes) **5–8 mm across**, in small, hanging clusters.

Where Found: Dry to moist, open sites; plains to subalpine; southern NWT to Colorado.

Notes: Pin cherry leaves, bark, wood and seeds (stones) contain hydrocyanic acid, and therefore can cause **cyanide poisoning**. Crushed leaves or thin strips of bark will kill insects in an enclosed space. The flesh of the cherry is the only edible part—the stone should always be discarded. • Pin cherries can be eaten raw, as a tart nibble, but usually they are cooked, strained and made into jelly or wine. The fruit seldom contains enough natural pectin to make a firm jelly, so additional pectin must be added. Pin cherries are still collected in large quantities today.

SASKATOON
Amelanchier alnifolia

General: Deciduous shrub or small tree, erect to spreading, 1–5 m tall; **branches smooth, dark grey** when mature, often spreads to form thickets.

Leaves: Alternate, oval to nearly round, 2–5 cm long, **rounded at tip, coarsely toothed on upper half**, green (often with a whitish bloom) in summer, yellowish-orange to reddish-brown in autumn.

Flowers: White, star-shaped, about 2 cm across, with 5 slender petals, 3–20 **in short, leafy clusters** (racemes) near branch tips; April to July.

Fruits: Berry-like pomes (**like tiny apples**), **purple to black with a whitish bloom** (dull red at first), juicy, 6–12 mm across.

Where Found: Open woods, banks and hillsides; plains to montane; Alaska to Colorado.

Notes: These sweet fruits were one of the most important berries for native peoples. They were eaten fresh, dried, or mashed and dried in cakes. Lewis and Clark reported that these 'cakes' could weigh as much as 7 kg. Dried fruits were often mixed with meat and fat or added to soups and stews. Today, they are used in pies, pancakes, puddings, muffins, jams, jellies, syrups and wine—much like blueberries. • The hard, strong, straight branches were a favourite material for making arrows and spears, and they were also used for canes, canoes (cross-pieces), basket rims, tipi stakes and tipi closure pins. • Saskatoons make excellent ornamental shrubs. They are hardy and easily propagated, and have beautiful, white blossoms in spring plus delicious fruit and scarlet leaves in autumn. • Deer, elk and moose browse on these shrubs; bears, chipmunks, squirrels and many birds feast on the seedy fruits. • Other common names include **Juneberry**, **serviceberry** and **shadbush**.

OCEANSPRAY; CREAMBUSH
Holodiscus discolor

General: Erect, deciduous shrub, 1–3 m tall; branches slender, arching, **slightly angled by leaf bases**, brownish and peeling with age.

Leaves: Alternate, **egg-shaped**, rounded, squared or wedge-shaped at base, **coarsely toothed or shallowly lobed**, usually 4–7 cm long, with 1–1.5 cm long stalks, green above, paler and more densely hairy beneath.

Flowers: Creamy white, saucer-shaped with 5 broad petals, about **5 mm across**; many flowers in **feathery, 10–17 cm long, branched clusters** (panicles); June to August.

Fruits: Hairy achenes about 2 mm long, persistent.

Where Found: Dry to moist, open or wooded sites; foothills to montane; southern BC to Idaho and Montana.

Notes: Mountainspray (***H. dumosus***) has smaller leaves with 1–2 cm long blades that taper to long, winged stalks. It grows on dry slopes in foothills and montane zones from Idaho and Wyoming to New Mexico. • Ninebark (p. 63) could be confused with oceanspray, but the bark of the two shrubs is quite different. Ninebark has loose and peeling bark, and oceanspray has ribbed branches and twigs. • The small, dry, flattened fruits of both species were eaten by some tribes. Mountainspray roots were used to make tea. • The wood is extremely hard, and it was used by the Thompson tribe to make breast-plates and other parts for armor. It was also used in arrow, spear and harpoon shafts, bows, digging sticks, tipi pins, fish clubs and drum hoops. • One Thompson name for oceanspray means 'disappearing-plant,' in reference to the fast appearance and disappearance of the flowers. The genus name *Holodiscus* comes from the Greek holo, 'whole,' and diskos, 'disc,' in reference to the unlobed or 'whole' disc surrounding the ovary.

THIMBLEBERRY
Rubus parviflorus

General: Deciduous shrub, erect, 0.5–2 m tall; **without prickles**, often form dense thickets from spreading rhizomes.

Leaves: Alternate, **maple-leaf–like**, palmately 3–7-lobed, **5–20 cm wide**, usually fuzzy-hairy above and beneath; stalks long and glandular.

Flowers: White, saucer-shaped, 2.5–5 cm across, with 5 broad, 'crinkled' petals, in long-stemmed, flat-topped clusters (panicles) of 3–7 at branch tips; May to July.

Fruits: Shallowly domed clusters of fleshy, red druplets, **raspberry-like**, dull, hairy, 15–20 mm wide.

Where Found: Open to wooded, moist to dry sites; foothills to montane; BC and Alberta to New Mexico.

Notes: Thimbleberries can be tasteless, tart or sweet, depending on the season and the habitat. They are fairly coarse and seedy, but most native groups ate these common berries. They are difficult to pick and because they do not dry or keep well, they were usually eaten fresh, rather than stored for winter. Young shoots can be peeled and eaten raw or cooked. • The large leaves were widely used as plates, containers, basket liners and toilet paper. • Bears and small birds enjoy these berries, and deer browse the plants. • The species name, *parviflorus*, from the Latin, *parvus*, 'small,' and *floris*, 'flower,' could refer to the few-flowered panicles, but certainly not to the size of these large blossoms.

WILD RED RASPBERRY
Rubus idaeus

General: Prickly, **erect to spreading** shrub, 50–200 cm tall, similar to a cultivated raspberry; **branches (canes) biennial**, green and bristly in 1st year, yellowish-brown to cinnamon-brown and with **straight, slender prickles** in 2nd year.

Leaves: Alternate, **palmately divided into 3–5 egg-shaped, pointed, double saw-toothed leaflets** each 4–10 cm long.

Flowers: White, 8–12 mm wide, with 5 glandular-hairy, backward-bending sepals, 5 slender, erect petals and 75–100 stamens, **nodding; many flowers in small clusters** (racemes) of 1–4 from upper leaf axils; June to July.

Fruits: Juicy, red druplets in dense clusters (raspberries) about 1 cm across.

Where Found: Moist to dry, open or wooded sites; foothills to montane; Alaska to New Mexico.

Notes: This species is also known as ***R. strigosus***. • **Black raspberry** (***R. leucodermis***) (lower photo) has thorny stems with a whitish bloom and flattened, hooked prickles. Its leaves are greyish-woolly beneath, and it produces large, flat-topped clusters of dark purple to black fruits on prickly stalks. Black raspberry grows on open or wooded slopes in the foothills from southern BC to Wyoming. • The tender, young shoots are edible when peeled of their bristly outer layer. Fresh or dried leaves make excellent tea, but **wilted leaves** can be **toxic**. This tea should be used in moderation, because extended use can irritate the stomach and bowels. • Raspberry tea has traditionally been given to women before, during and after childbirth. Pharmacologists have validated the use of raspberry leaf as an antispasmodic for treating painful menstruation. It contains 'fragarine,' a compound that acts both as a relaxant and a stimulant on the muscles of the uterus. Modern-day 'Motherese' tablets contain extracts of raspberry leaves.

SHRUBBY CINQUEFOIL
Pentaphylloides floribunda

General: Deciduous shrub, erect to spreading, 10–100 cm tall (sometimes to 150 cm); branches numerous, with **shredding, reddish-brown bark** when mature.

Leaves: Alternate, pinnately compound, with **3–7 (usually 5)** linear to oblong, **crowded leaflets**, 1–2 cm long, **greyish-green**, silky.

Flowers: Yellow, **buttercup-like**, 1.5–3 cm across, with 5 broad petals, 1–7 in small clusters (cymes) at branch tips; June to August.

Fruits: Light brown achenes, densely covered with long, white, straight hairs, about 1.5–1.8 mm long, numerous.

Where Found: Wet to dry, often rocky sites; plains to subalpine; Alaska to New Mexico.

Notes: This species is also known as ***Potentilla fruticosa***. • **Apache plume** (***Fallugia paradoxa***) is a low, finely branched shrub with pinnately cut leaves (but lobed, not divided into leaflets) and small, rose-like flowers (but white, not yellow). It has pale, whitish bark and its flowers produce fluffy heads of seeds, with each seed bearing a 2.5–5 cm long tail. Apache plume is common on dry slopes in plains, foothills and montane zones from southern Colorado to Utah and New Mexico. • The thin, dry, papery strips of bark were used as tinder, in the days when fires were started by twirling sticks. • This attractive shrub is used for erosion control, especially along highways. Cuttings root readily in sand, and the mature shrubs are very hardy. • Ungulates generally prefer to eat other plants, but they will browse shrubby cinquefoil when more desirable plants are absent. Heavily browsed cinquefoils indicate overgrazing, by either wild or domestic animals, suggesting a need to reduce the number of animals in an area.

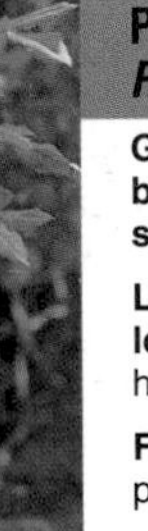

PRICKLY ROSE
Rosa acicularis

General: Deciduous shrub, erect to spreading, 20–120 cm tall; **branches densely covered with weak, bristly prickles and straight, slender thorns**; often forming colonies from underground stems.

Leaves: Alternate, pinnately compound, usually with **5–7 oblong leaflets,** each about 3–4 cm long**, sharply double-toothed**, somewhat hairy beneath.

Flowers: Pink, saucer-shaped, 5–7 cm across, with 5 broad, single petals; flowers on short branches; June to August.

Fruits: Scarlet, round to pear-shaped, berry-like 'hips,' 1.5–3 cm long, with a fleshy outer layer enclosing many stiff-hairy achenes.

Where Found: Open to wooded, dry to moist sites; plains to subalpine; Alaska to New Mexico.

Notes: Prairie rose (***R. woodsii***) (bottom photo) is very similar, but it has clusters of round, small (6–12 mm long) hips. It lacks numerous, bristly prickles; instead, it has larger thorns at its nodes. It grows in a wide range of habitats from the plains to subalpine zones, from the southern Yukon and NWT to Colorado and Utah. • **Nootka rose** (***R. nutkana***) is very similar to prairie rose, but it has larger flowers (about 8 cm across) and fruits (about 2 cm long) that are usually solitary. It grows in a wide range of foothills and montane zones from southern BC to Colorado and Utah. • Most parts of rose shrubs are edible. The hips remain on the branches through winter, so they are available for food when most other fruits have gone. They are rich in vitamins A, B, C, E and K. Usually only the fleshy outer layer is eaten, because the dry inner seeds (achenes) are not palatable, and their sliver-like hairs can **irritate** the digestive tract and cause 'itchy bum' on their way out. Some tribes considered rose hips to be 'famine food.' • Prickly rose is the floral emblem of Alberta.

WESTERN MOUNTAIN-ASH
Sorbus scopulina

General: Deciduous shrub, clumped, erect to spreading, 1–4 m tall; branches slightly white-hairy and sticky when young, reddish-grey to yellowish when mature.

Leaves: Alternate, pinnately compound with 11–13 leaflets; leaflets elliptic, **sharp-tipped**, 3–6 cm long, **sharply toothed from tip to base**, glossy green.

Flowers: White, saucer-shaped, about 1 cm across, with 5 broad petals; **70–200 in flat-topped clusters** (corymbs) 9–15 cm across; June to July.

Fruits: Glossy, orange to scarlet, berry-like pomes, 7–8 mm long, in dense clusters.

Where Found: Moist, open or shaded sites; foothills to subalpine; the Yukon and NWT to New Mexico.

Notes: Sitka mountain-ash (***S. sitchensis***) has 7–11 bluish-green, round-tipped leaflets that are toothed mainly above the middle. It has non-sticky twigs, rusty hairs and red berries. Sitka mountain-ash grows in foothills, montane and subalpine zones from BC and Alberta to Montana. • Some tribes ate these bitter fruits, fresh or dried, but many considered them inedible. Today, they are usually made into jams and jellies. • Native peoples boiled the peeled branches or inner bark to make teas for treating back pain, colds, headaches, sore chests and internal bleeding (perhaps associated with tuberculosis). The branches were boiled, and then the steam was inhaled to relieve headaches and sore chests. • This species makes an attractive garden shrub. It is easily propagated from seed sown in autumn. The scarlet fruit clusters draw many birds.

S. sitchensis

CREEPING OREGON-GRAPE; CREEPING MAHONIA
Mahonia repens

General: Low, wintergreen shrub; branches erect or prostrate, 10–30 cm long; **bud scales less than 1 cm** long, soon falling; often spreading by rhizomes.

Leaves: Alternate, pinnately compound, usually with **5–7 leaflets edged with spine-tipped teeth (holly-like)**, leathery, dull or glossy, green above, dull with whitish bloom beneath, red or purple in winter; leaflets oblong to egg-shaped, 3–8 cm long.

Flowers: Yellow, about 1 cm across, with 6 petals and 6 sepals; in elongated, **many-flowered clusters** (racemes); April to June.

Fruits: Grape-like, juicy berries about 7–8 mm long, purplish-blue with a whitish bloom and few large seeds.

Where Found: Forested slopes; foothills to montane; southern BC and Alberta to New Mexico.

Notes: This species is also known as ***Berberis repens*** and can also be called **holly-grape**. • **Tall Oregon-grape** (***M. aquifolium***) is similar to creeping Oregon-grape but it is much taller (30–150 cm). Its leaflets have prominent spines, and they are always shiny above and not whitened beneath. Tall Oregon-grape grows on open or wooded slopes in the foothills of southern BC, Idaho and Montana. • **Dull Oregon-grape** (***M. nervosa***) (lower photo) can be identified by its longer leaves (9–19 leaflets) and larger (2–4 cm long), leathery bud scales. This prostrate shrub grows on forested slopes in the foothills of BC and Idaho. • The juicy berries make good jelly, jam and wine. They can be eaten raw, but they are quite sour. The juice, sweetened with sugar, tastes much like grape juice. • The roots contain the alkaloid 'berberis,' which stimulates involuntary muscles. The Flathead used root tea to aid in delivery of the placenta. Crushed plants and root tea are antiseptic and antibacterial, and they were used to aid healing of wounds. The leaf tea was taken as a tonic and as a contraceptive, and was also used to treat kidney troubles, stomach troubles, rheumatism and loss of appetite. The National Standard Dispensatory lists many uses, but it also warns that **an overdose can be fatal**.

SNOWBRUSH; VELVETY BUCKBRUSH
Ceanothus velutinus

General: Sprawling, spicy-scented, evergreen shrub, usually 50–300 cm tall; twigs olive-green; usually **in dense patches**.

Leaves: Alternate, **broadly oval**, 4–8 cm long, **finely toothed**, with **3 prominent veins** from base, **shiny, often sticky above**, finely greyish-hairy beneath; stipules 1 mm long.

Flowers: White, tiny, star-shaped, with 5 slender, cupped petals and 5 tiny sepals; many flowers in **several dense, pyramid-shaped clusters** (cymes) at tips of side branches, fragrant; June to August.

Fruits: Glandular-sticky, deeply 3-lobed capsules, 4–5 mm long, with a **small crest on each lobe**, ejecting 3 shiny seeds when mature.

Where Found: Moist to dry, open or fairly open sites; foothills to montane; BC and Alberta to Colorado.

Notes: Fendler's buckbrush (***C. fendleri***) is a low (10–50 cm tall), spiny shrub with small (1–3 cm long), toothless leaves and small, umbrella-shaped clusters (umbels) of white flowers. It grows on dry slopes in foothills and montane zones from Wyoming to New Mexico. • **Red-stemmed buckbrush** (***C. sanguineus***) has thinner, deciduous leaves that are sometimes shiny and sticky. Its stipules are 3–8 mm long and the lobes of its capsules are rounded (never crested). It grows on well-drained, open or wooded slopes in the foothills of southern BC, Idaho and Montana. • The abundant, fire-resistant seeds can survive in the soil for at least 200 years before fire stimulates them to germinate. Young shrubs grow rapidly in open (recently burned) sites, but they are eventually shaded out by trees. However, their seeds remain, ready to start a new shrub community after the next forest fire. • Deer, elk and moose eat this shrub and birds eat the seeds.

C. sanguineus

ALDER-LEAVED BUCKTHORN
Rhamnus alnifolia

General: Erect or spreading shrub, 50–150 cm tall; branches finely grey-hairy, hairless and dark grey-brown with age.

Leaves: Alternate, lance- to egg-shaped, 3–10 cm long, thin, with **5–7 prominent side veins, finely glandular-toothed**, short-stalked.

Flowers: Greenish-yellow, cupped, **5 mm wide**, with 5 sepals and no petals, **2–5 in small clusters** (umbels) from lower leaf axils; all male or female on 1 plant; June to July.

Fruits: Reddish to bluish-black, berry-like drupes, 6–8 mm long, with 3 flat nutlets.

Where Found: Moist to wet, shady sites; foothills to montane; BC and Alberta to Wyoming.

Notes: Cascara (***Frangula purshiana***, also known as ***R. purshiana***) (lower photo) is a larger shrub or small tree, up to 10 m tall. Its leaves have 10–12 side veins, and its flowers are borne in larger, 8–40-flowered, stalked clusters. Cascara grows on wooded slopes in the foothills of BC, Idaho and Montana. • These berries are **poisonous**. • The bark of alder-leaved buckthorn contains a laxative, but cascara, 'the all-American laxative,' is much more widely used. Native peoples collected the bark in spring and summer, either by scraping downwards (if the patient needed a laxative) or upwards (if the patient needed to vomit). It was then dried and stored for later use. Fresh bark can have very severe effects, but curing it for at least 1 year reduces its harshness. The bark was used to make medicinal teas, but today it is usually administered as a liquid extract or elixir or in tablet form. Each year, 0.5–1.4 million kg of bark are collected, mainly from wild shrubs in BC, Washington, Oregon and California forests.

RED-OSIER DOGWOOD
Cornus sericea

General: Deciduous shrub, erect to spreading, 0.5–3 m tall, often clumped; **branches opposite, purple to red** (sometimes greenish).

Leaves: Opposite, egg- to lance-shaped, 2–10 cm long, pointed, **with 5–7 prominent, parallel veins that converge towards tip**, red in autumn.

Flowers: White, about 5 mm across, in dense, **flat-topped clusters** (cymes), 2–5 cm across at branch tips; May to July.

Fruits: White (sometimes bluish), **berry-like** drupes with large, flattened stones, 5–7 mm across, juicy.

Where Found: Moist, wooded to open sites; plains to montane; the southern Yukon and NWT to New Mexico.

Notes: This species is also known as ***C. alba***, ***C. stolonifera*** and ***Svida sericea***. • The fruits are very bitter to modern-day tastes, but native peoples collected them for food in the past. Usually they were mixed with other sweeter berries or with sugar to make 'sweet-and-sour.' • The soft, white inner bark was dried and used for smoking, either alone or mixed with tobacco or kinnikinnick. • The flexible branches are often used in basket weaving, especially for making attractive, red rims. • This shrub is very attractive, with lush green leaves and white flowers in spring and with red branches and white berries in winter. It grows best in moist sites and is easily propagated from cuttings or by layering. • Red-osier dogwood is browsed by moose and other ungulates, and birds and bears enjoy the bitter, white berries.

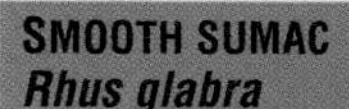

SMOOTH SUMAC
Rhus glabra

General: Deciduous shrub, 1–2 m tall; branches few, smooth, usually hairless; often **forming thickets** from shallow, spreading roots.

Leaves: Alternate, pinnately divided into **11–21 lance-shaped, 5–12 cm long leaflets**, toothed, green above, pale with a whitish bloom beneath, **bright red in autumn**.

Flowers: Cream-coloured to greenish-yellow, about 3 mm across, cup-shaped with 5 spreading, fuzzy petals, **in dense, pyramid-shaped clusters (panicles) 10–20 cm long**; April to July.

Fruits: Densely reddish-hairy, berry-like drupes, 4–5 mm long, in persistent, fuzzy clusters.

Where Found: Dry slopes; plains and foothills; southern BC to New Mexico.

Notes: Squawbush (***R. trilobata***), also called **skunkbush**, is a strong-smelling, 1–2 m tall, rounded shrub. Its bright green leaves are divided into 3 broad-tipped, lobed leaflets that taper to wedge-shaped bases. Its small, dense flower clusters appear before the leaves, and they produce fuzzy, reddish-orange fruits. Squawbush grows along streams on plains and foothills from Idaho and Alberta to New Mexico. • The fuzzy, red fruits of smooth sumac can be crushed, soaked in cold water, and strained to produce a pink or rose-coloured drink that is sweetened with sugar and served cold. • All parts of this shrub were used to make medicinal teas for treating anything from tuberculosis and gonorrhea to itchy skin. • Squawbush fruits were eaten raw, or sometimes ground with a little water. They were often mixed with other foods, especially sugar and roasted corn. The inner bark was also eaten. • Squawbush branches were split lengthwise (usually 3 times) and woven into baskets and water bottles. Sun shades or hats were woven from the smaller branches, but these were for adults only. It was said that if a child placed a sumac on his head, he would stop growing.

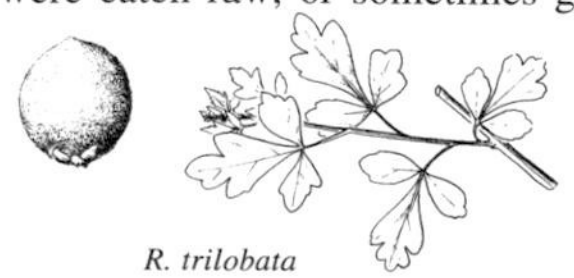

R. trilobata

POISON-IVY
Toxicodendron radicans

General: Trailing to erect, deciduous shrub, **usually 10–25 cm tall** (sometimes clambering to 200 cm), often forms **colonies from creeping rhizomes**.

Leaves: Alternate, divided into **3 egg-shaped, pointed leaflets** 3–15 cm long, prominently veined beneath, long-stalked, **glossy and bright green, scarlet in autumn**.

Flowers: Cream-coloured, 4–5 mm across, cup-shaped with 5 spreading petals; **in crowded clusters (panicles)** from leaf axils; May to July.

Fruits: White or yellowish-white, smooth, **berry-like drupes**, 5–7 mm wide.

Where Found: Well-drained, open or shaded sites; plains to foothills; BC and Alberta to New Mexico.

Notes: This species has also been called ***Rhus radicans*** and ***T. rydbergii.*** • Poison-ivy plants contain a resin that causes a **nasty skin reaction** in most people. It is not volatile, and therefore it is not transmitted through the air, but it can be carried to unsuspecting victims on pets, clothing and tools, and even on smoke particles from burning poison-ivy plants. The resin can be removed by washing with a strong soap shortly after contact (5–10 minutes), but usually people do not realize that they had come in contact with this plant until it is too late. The Navajo rubbed sheep blood over affected skin. Ointments and even household ammonia can be used to relieve the itching of mild cases, but people with severe reactions may need to consult a doctor. • In southern California, some tribes mashed poison-ivy leaves and applied this as a cure for ringworm. • Among the Navajo, gamblers were allowed to use poisonous plants, and poison-ivy was no exception. It was considered 'good luck' to chew a small piece of these leaves and then give it to your opponent, but it seems unlikely that either player would benefit from this exchange.

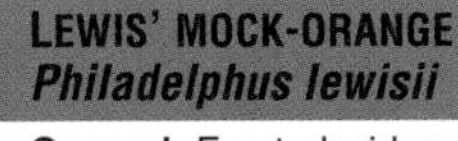

LEWIS' MOCK-ORANGE
Philadelphus lewisii

General: Erect, deciduous shrub, 1–3 m tall; **branches opposite,** loose, spreading, with brown, flaky bark.

Leaves: Opposite, **lance- to egg-shaped, 2.5–7 cm long**, with **3 main veins** from base, slightly rough to touch, fringed with short, curved hairs.

Flowers: White, about **3 cm across, cross-shaped**, with 4 broad, rounded or notched, spreading petals around a cluster of 25–40 bright yellow stamens, 3–11 in showy clusters (racemes) at branch tips, **fragrant**; May to July.

Fruits: Woody, **oval capsules, 6–10 mm long**, splitting into 4 parts (valves), with many rod-shaped seeds.

Where Found: Well-drained sites, often along streams; foothills to montane; BC and Alberta to Idaho and Montana.

Notes: Littleleaf mock-orange (***P. microphyllus***) has smaller (1–3 cm long), shiny, leathery leaves and its flowers are usually single. It grows on dry, rocky slopes in the foothills from Wyoming to New Mexico. • Lewis' mock-orange is the state flower of Idaho. • The stiff, hard wood has been used to make combs, knitting needles, rims for birch-bark baskets and cradle hoods. The wood was burned and the charcoal was then ground and mixed with pitch or bear grease to make salves for treating sores and swellings. Powdered leaves were used in a similar way. Women bruised the fresh leaves and used them as poultices to heal infected breasts. Branches, with or without blossoms, were boiled to make a medicinal tea to wash or soak eczema and bleeding hemorrhoids. It was also drunk to treat a sore chest. • Mock-orange leaves were mashed and used as soap.

SILVERBERRY; WOLFWILLOW
Elaeagnus commutata

General: Erect shrub, 1–5 m tall; small branches densely covered with **rusty-brown scales**; often forming colonies from extensive spreading rhizomes.

Leaves: Alternate, egg- or **lance-shaped**, usually **2–6 cm long** (sometimes to 10 cm), **silvery** with dense, tiny, star-shaped hairs, sometimes also with **brown scales beneath**.

Flowers: Yellow within, silvery without, funnel-shaped, 12–16 mm long, with 4 spreading, pointed lobes, in 2s or 3s from leaf axils, **strongly sweet-scented**; June to July.

Fruits: Silvery, dry, mealy, oval, about 1 cm long, drupe-like, with a single large nutlet.

Where Found: Well-drained, open sites; plains to montane; Alaska to Idaho and Montana.

Notes: These flowers can be detected from metres away by their sweet, heavy perfume. Some people enjoy this fragrance, but others find it overwhelming. If green silverberry wood is put on the fire, it gives off a strong smell of human excrement. Some practical jokers enjoy sneaking branches into the fire and watching the reactions of fellow campers. • Some northern tribes ate silverberries, but many groups considered the dry, mealy berries only as famine food. The berries were mixed with blood and cooked, mixed with lard and eaten raw, frozen like ice cream, or fried in moose fat. Apparently, silverberries make good jam. • The bark was used to make cord, and several tribes used the nutlets inside the 'berries' as decorative beads. The fruits were boiled to remove the flesh, and while the seeds were still soft, a hole was made through each. They were then threaded, dried, oiled, and polished.

CANADA BUFFALOBERRY; SOOPOLALLIE
Shepherdia canadensis

General: Deciduous shrub, spreading, 1–2 m tall; branches **opposite, brownish, with small, bran-like scabs** when young.

Leaves: Opposite, oval, 1.5–6 cm long, **dark green above, fuzzy beneath with silvery, star-shaped hairs and rust-coloured scales**.

Flowers: Yellowish to greenish, inconspicuous, about 4 mm wide, male or female and with sexes on separate plants, in small clusters below new leaves; April to June, appearing before leaves.

Fruits: Bright red to yellowish berries, 4–6 mm long, juicy and translucent, soapy to touch.

Where Found: Open woods and streambanks; foothills to subalpine; Alaska to New Mexico.

Notes: These berries were collected by beating the branches over a canvas or hide with a stick. They were then eaten fresh or dried for future use. Buffaloberries contain a bitter substance (saponin) that makes the juice soapy to the touch and foamy when beaten—hence another common name, **soapberry**. They were whipped like egg-whites to make a foamy dessert called 'Indian ice cream.' This is rather bitter for modern-day tastes, but it can be sweetened with sugar or with other berries. Buffaloberries were also added to stews or cooked to make syrup, sauce or jelly. • The berries are rich in vitamin C and iron, but large amounts can cause **diarrhea, vomiting** and **cramps**. • After giving up its bark for strings and its berries for fruit, the buffaloberry refused to give up its wood. Some tribes called it 'stinkwood,' and if you burn it you will understand why. • The genus name, *Shepherdia*, commemorates John Shepherd, an English botanist who lived from 1764–1836.

FALSEBOX; MOUNTAIN BOXWOOD
Paxistima myrsinites

General: Evergreen shrub, erect to prostrate, 20–60 cm tall; with many branches, **4-sided, reddish-brown**.

Leaves: Opposite (or nearly so), elliptic to oval, 1–3 cm long, **glossy, leathery, thick, sharply toothed**.

Flowers: Greenish-brown to **dark reddish**, fragrant, 3–4 mm across, with 4 petals; many flowers in small clusters (cymes) of 1–few **along branches in leaf axils**; May to August.

Fruits: Oval capsules, 3–4 mm long, with 1–2 dark seeds usually with a **whitish, fleshy coating**.

Where Found: Moist forests to well-drained, open sites; foothills to subalpine; southern BC and Alberta to New Mexico.

Notes: Falsebox leaves were boiled slightly and used in poultices for healing swellings and reducing pain. Tea made from the leaves was taken to treat tuberculosis and to heal broken bones and internal problems. • The branches are used as greenery in flower arrangements—to the extent that some areas near urban centres have been depleted of these shrubs by people gathering branches for florists. • Deer and elk browse on these shrubs. • The genus name, *Paxistima* (also spelled ***Pachistima***), was derived from the Greek, *pachus*, 'thick,' and *stigma*, 'stigma,' referring to the thick stigmas of these flowers. You can easily remember it by repeating the phrase, 'Pa kissed ma.'

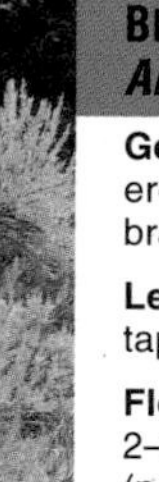

BIG SAGEBRUSH
Artemisia tridentata

General: Greyish, wintergreen shrub, **aromatic**, much branched, erect, usually 0.5–2 m tall; bark greyish and shredding on older branches, densely hairy on young twigs.

Leaves: Alternate, **narrowly wedge-shaped, 3-toothed at tip** and tapered to base, 1–2 cm long, densely grey-hairy.

Flowerheads: Small, yellow or brownish heads of 5–8 disc florets, 2–3 mm across; numerous flowerheads in **long, narrow clusters** (panicles) 1.5–7 cm wide; July to October.

Fruits: Sparsely hairy achenes; no pappus.

Where Found: Dry plains and slopes, often covering many hectares; plains to montane; southern BC and Alberta to New Mexico.

Notes: Threetip sagebrush (***A. tripartita***) also has greyish, fragrant, 3-lobed, wedge-shaped leaves, but it is usually a much smaller shrub (20–60 cm tall), and the 3 lobes at its leaf tips are long and linear. Three-tip sagebrush grows in dry habitats in plains to montane zones from BC and Montana to Colorado. • **Silver sagebrush** (***A. cana***) is a gnarled, 30–150 cm tall shrub with unlobed, linear to lance-shaped leaves that are 1–4 cm long and covered with silvery and greyish, woolly hairs. It grows on dry plains and slopes in the foothills and montane zones from BC and Alberta to Colorado. • **Antelopebrush** (***Purshia tridentata***), also known as **bitterbrush**, could be mistaken for big sagebrush, because it has very similar (but not aromatic) leaves. However, it is a member of the rose family (Rosaceae), distinguished by its small, bright yellow, rose-like flowers (produced in early summer) and its velvety, spindle-shaped, 1.5 cm long achenes. Antelopebrush grows on dry sites in the plains and foothills from southern BC and Alberta to New Mexico. • Although they can be quite bitter, the seeds of several sagebrushes were used for food, and those of big sagebrush were considered the best. They were eaten raw or dried, often ground into meal and cooked. • Livestock do not like to eat big sagebrush, and overgrazing of grasslands can result in dramatic increases in the abundance of this shrub. • Big sagebrush is usually killed by fire, but threetip sagebrush re-sprouts readily after a burn.

COMMON RABBITBUSH
Chrysothamnus nauseosus

General: Erect, deciduous shrub, usually 20–60 cm tall (sometimes over 1 m), **densely branched, often flat-topped**; branches flexible, covered with grey, felt-like hairs.

Leaves: Alternate, **linear**, 3–6 cm long, about 1 mm wide, **grey-velvety**, not much twisted.

Flowerheads: Small, **yellow** heads of 5 disc florets, about 5 mm across; many flowerheads **in dense clusters (cymes) at branch tips**; involucral bracts rounded or abruptly pointed, **not green-tipped**; August to October.

Fruits: Hairy, linear achenes; pappus of white hairs.

Where Found: Dry, open sites; plains to montane; southern BC and Alberta to New Mexico.

Notes: Rabbitbush species are highly variable, and the common species in the Rocky Mountains all have many varieties or subspecies that are not described here. • **Parry's rabbitbush** (***C. parryi***) is very similar to common rabbitbush, but the bracts of its involucres have slender, green, herbaceous tips. It grows on dry slopes and in open forests from the plains to subalpine zones from Wyoming to Colorado. • **Green rabbitbush** (***C. viscidiflorus***) has brittle twigs that are hairless or only slightly hairy (not felt-like). It grows in dry, open sites in the plains, foothills and montane zones from southern BC to New Mexico. • **Grey horsebrush** (***Tetradymia canescens***) is a small shrub (20–60 cm tall) with narrow, white-felted leaves. Its small, yellow flowerheads each have 4 hairy, whitish involucral bracts and 4 slender-lobed disc florets. It grows on dry, open sites on the plains and foothills from southern BC and Montana to New Mexico. • Rabbitbush branches were burned slowly to smoke hides, and boughs were used to cover and carpet sweathouses. Mature flowers were boiled for at least 6 hours to produce a lemon-yellow dye for wool, leather and baskets. The inclusion of immature buds or twigs gave the dye a greenish tinge.

C. viscidiflorus *C. parryi* *C. nauseosus* *T. canescens*

TRAPPER'S TEA; GLANDULAR LABRADOR TEA
Ledum glandulosum

General: Evergreen shrub, 40–80 cm tall (sometimes to150 cm); branches with tiny hairs and glandular dots.

Leaves: Alternate, **elliptic to oval**, 1.5–4 cm long, **leathery, slightly rolled under**, green above, **pale with dense resin glands and short, white (not brown), scaly hairs beneath**, often bent downwards.

Flowers: White, 1–1.5 cm across, with 5 broad, spreading petals and 8–12 long stamens, in **clusters (corymbs) at branch tips**; June to August.

Fruits: Nodding, rounded capsules, 3–5 mm long, short-hairy and glandular, on 1–2 cm long stalks.

Where Found: Moist to wet, open or wooded sites; montane to subalpine; BC and Alberta to Wyoming.

Notes: Labrador tea (***L. groenlandicum***) (lower photo) is easily distinguished from trapper's tea by the rusty-brown hairs on the lower side of its leaves. It grows in boggy sites in foothills, montane, subalpine and alpine zones from Alaska to southern BC and Alberta. • Trapper's tea contains the **poisonous alkaloid** andromedotoxin, which is toxic to livestock, especially sheep. • Tea can be brewed from both species, but trapper's tea must be boiled for a long time, to destroy any harmful alkaloids. These teas should be used in moderation to avoid drowsiness. Excessive amounts are said to stimulate urination and bowel movements, and to cause intestinal disturbances. Do not confuse these tea plants with the poisonous bog-laurels (p. 76).

SMALL BOG-LAUREL; SWAMP-LAUREL
Kalmia microphylla

General: Evergreen shrub, 5–20 cm tall; many slender branches; often forming mats from low-spreading branches and short rhizomes.

Leaves: Opposite, 1–2 cm long, oval to elliptic-oblong, less than twice as long as wide, usually rolled under at edges, **leathery, dark glossy green** above, whitish with fine hairs beneath.

Flowers: Rose-pink, saucer-shaped, 2–12 mm across, with 5 shallow lobes, in loose clusters (corymbs) at stem tips; June to September.

Fruits: Round capsules, splitting into 5 pieces (valves).

Where Found: Moist to wet, open sites; subalpine to alpine; the Yukon and NWT to Colorado.

Notes: This species is also known as ***K. polifolia* var. *microphylla*** and **var. *occidentalis***. • **Glossy bog-laurel** (***K. polifolia***, also called ***K. polifolia* var. *polifolia***) is very similar to small bog-laurel, and some taxonomists classify these 2 plants as varieties of the same species. Glossy bog-laurel is a taller plant (usually 30–40 cm) with larger flowers (12–18 mm wide), and its leaves are longer (2–4 cm) and narrower (usually over twice as long as wide). It grows in peat bogs in montane and subalpine zones from the Yukon and NWT to Alberta. • Bog laurels contain **poisonous alkaloids**. When they are not in flower, they could be confused with Labrador tea or trapper's tea (p. 75), but the leaves of those shrubs have brownish hairs on their undersides, or they are much narrower. • Each anther is neatly tucked into a small, dimpled pocket in a petal, and held there under tension. At the slightest touch from an insect, the stamens pop up, dusting the visitor with pollen, which is then carried to the next flower. A gentle prod with a straw will have the same effect.

FOUR-ANGLED MOUNTAIN-HEATHER
Cassiope tetragona

General: Tufted, evergreen shrub, usually **5–15 cm tall**; branches covered with dense, scale-like, overlapping leaves, **appear 4-sided**; often forming large colonies from spreading stems.

Leaves: Opposite, in 4 vertical rows, thick, stalkless, scale-like, 2–5 mm long, with a **prominent groove** on the upper side, minutely hairy, dark green.

Flowers: White, sometimes rose-tinged, **bell-shaped**, 4–7 mm long, **nodding** on 10–25 mm long stalks from upper leaf axils; June to August.

Fruits: Round capsules with many seeds.

Where Found: Moist slopes; subalpine to alpine; Alaska to Montana.

Notes: White mountain-heather (***C. mertensiana***) is very similar to four-angled mountain-heather, but its leaves do not have a groove on the outer side, and they are essentially hairless. It grows on moist slopes in subalpine and alpine zones from BC and Alberta to Montana. • Mountain-heather plants (*Phyllodoce* spp. and *Cassiope* spp.) have been used to make a bitter-tasting medicinal tea for treating tuberculosis. This treatment was discovered by an Okanagan man suffering from tuberculosis, who travelled to the mountains with some berry pickers. While there, he fell asleep in a patch of mountain-heather and dreamed of a cure. When he awoke, he boiled the heather plants and drank the tea. He continued this for some time and eventually regained his health. • These plants survive the rigors of arctic and alpine environments by growing in moist depressions, where they remain covered by snow in winter. Their nodding, bell-shaped flowers trap warm air rising from the ground; on still, sunny days, they can average 3.7° C warmer inside than out. These slow-growing plants can live for many years. They produce only a few new leaves each year, which live for 4–5 seasons.

PINK MOUNTAIN-HEATHER
Phyllodoce empetriformis

General: Dwarf, evergreen shrub, 10–40 cm tall; branches numerous, **glandular-hairy** when young; often forming mats.

Leaves: Alternate, **crowded in a bottlebrush-like arrangement, needle-like,** 5–12 mm long, grooved on lower side.

Flowers: Pink to deep rose, **bell-shaped**, 5–8 mm long, with rolled back lobes at edge; erect or nodding; **1–many flowers in umbel-like clusters at stem tips**; June to August.

Fruits: Erect, round capsules, about 4 mm across, open by slits at tip.

Where Found: Moist to wet, open sites; subalpine to alpine; the Yukon and NWT to Idaho, Montana and possibly Colorado.

Notes: Pink mountain-heather could be mistaken for **crowberry** (***Empetrum nigrum***) (middle photo), but crowberry has shorter leaves (3–7 mm long) and smaller, less-showy flowers, and it produces juicy black berries. • **Yellow mountain-heather** (***P. glanduliflora***) (bottom photo) has urn-shaped, yellowish-green flowers that are sticky with glandular hairs. It grows in moist, subalpine to alpine habitats from the Yukon and NWT to Wyoming. These 2 mountain-heathers often produce hybrids with pale pink flowers. • Pink mountain-heather is a popular rock garden plant. It is easily propagated from cuttings or by layering in sand. • The thick, needle-like leaves and low growth form help these dwarf shrubs to minimize water loss through evaporation. Frozen soil and cold, dry winds limit the amount of moisture available to plants in alpine habitats.

COMMON BEARBERRY; KINNIKINNICK
Arctostaphylos uva-ursi

General: Trailing, evergreen shrub, 5–15 cm tall; branches brownish-red to grey, peeling, flexible, rooting, 50–100 cm long, **form mats**.

Leaves: Alternate, **spoon-shaped, rounded at tip**, tapered to base, 1–3 cm long, **dark green and glossy** above, paler beneath, hairless.

Flowers: Pinkish to white, urn-shaped, 4–6 mm long, in small hanging clusters (racemes) at branch tips; May to June.

Fruits: Bright red, berry-like drupes, 6–10 mm across.

Where Found: Well-drained, open or wooded sites; foothills to alpine; Alaska to New Mexico.

Notes: Greenleaf manzanita (***A. patula***) is an erect shrub (usually over 1 m tall) with smooth, reddish branches, large (2–5 cm long), ovate, evergreen, yellow-green leaves and white to yellowish berries. It grows on wooded slopes from the plains to montane zones of western Colorado and Utah. • **Alpine bearberry** (***A. rubra***) (lower photo) has thin, veiny, toothed, deciduous leaves that often turn red in autumn. Its small, bell-shaped flowers produce juicy, red berries that are popular with many birds and mammals, including bears and the occasional hiker. It grows on moist slopes in montane, subalpine and alpine zones from Alaska to BC and Alberta. • The berries of common bearberry are edible, but they are mealy and tasteless. Native peoples ate them cooked and mixed with grease or fish eggs, to reduce the dryness. Syrup or sugar often added sweetness. Too many of these berries can cause constipation. • Common bearberry is widely used to make tea, but extended use can lead to **stomach** and **liver problems** (especially in children) and strong tea can bring on **uterine contractions** in pregnant women. • Common bearberry leaves were widely smoked, either alone or as a tobacco extender. The leaves are high in tannin, and they have been used to tan hides. • The genus name, from the Greek *arctos*, 'bear,' and *staphylos*, 'a bunch of grapes,' and the species name, from the Greek *uva*, 'grape,' and *ursus*, 'bear,' both mean 'bearberry.' Bears are very fond of this fruit.

PRINCE'S-PINE; PIPSISSEWA
Chimaphila umbellata

General: Evergreen shrub, **semi-woody**, erect, 10–30 cm tall, from spreading rhizomes.

Leaves: In **whorls of 3–8, narrowly spoon-shaped**, gradually tapered to base, 2–8 cm long, **sharply toothed, dark green and glossy** above, pale beneath.

Flowers: Light **pink** or rose-tinged, **waxy, saucer-shaped**, about 1 cm across, nodding; in erect clusters (corymbs) of 3–8, well above the leaves; June to August.

Fruits: Round capsules, 5–7 mm across, open from tip, **in erect clusters** above leaves.

Where Found: Wooded (usually coniferous) sites; foothills to montane; BC and Alberta to Colorado.

Notes: Menzies' pipsissewa (*C. menziesii*) is a smaller plant (5–15 cm tall) with fewer flowers (1–3) and with leaves that are broadest below (rather than above) the middle. It grows in coniferous forests from BC to Idaho and Montana. • Prince's-pine has been used to flavour candy, soft drinks (especially root beer) and traditional beers. • Native peoples ate the leaves raw or boiled with the roots as a tonic rich in vitamin C. Pipsissewa tea was used as a remedy for fluid retention, kidney or bladder problems and fever and coughs. Studies indicate that it increases urine flow and has astringent properties, so it should be useful for treating kidney infections.

C. menziesii

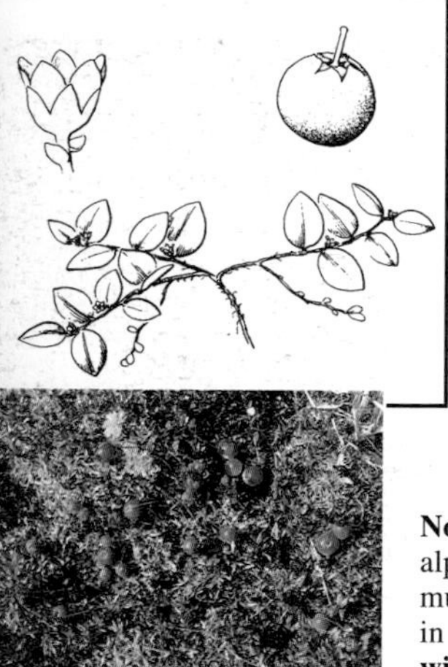

ALPINE FALSE-WINTERGREEN; TRAILING FALSE-WINTERGREEN
Gaultheria humifusa

General: Creeping, evergreen shrublet, 1–3 cm tall, hairless; branches slender, trailing, 5–10 cm long, often forming mats.

Leaves: Alternate, broadly egg-shaped to elliptic, **1–2 cm long, glossy, dark green, leathery** with thickened edges.

Flowers: Pinkish or greenish-white, bell-shaped, 3–4 mm long with 5 small lobes, single, from upper leaf axils; **calyx hairless**; July to August.

Fruits: Scarlet, pulpy, berry-like capsule, 5–6 mm wide.

Where Found: Moist to wet, open sites; subalpine to alpine; BC and Alberta to Colorado.

Notes: Slender false-wintergreen (***G. ovatifolia***) is very similar to alpine wintergreen, but it has hairy calyxes and its leaves are usually much larger (2–5 cm long). It grows on dry slopes and occasionally in bogs in subalpine zones in BC, Idaho and Montana. • **Hairy false-wintergreen** (***G. hispidula***), also called **creeping-snowberry**, is a smaller shrublet, with 4–10 mm long leaves, 4-lobed, white flowers, white berries and st ff, reddish-hairy stems. It grows in bogs and damp montane woods in BC, Alberta and Idaho. • Hairy false-wintergreen could be confused with a bog cranberry (***Oxycoccos*** spp.) (lower photo) at 1st glance, but bog cranberries have no stiff, reddish-brown hairs. When in bloom, bog cranberries have distinctive, tiny, shootingstar-like flowers, and these develop into large cranberries. **Bog cranberry** (***Oxycoccus quadripetalus***) has long leaves (6–11 mm), minutely hairy flower stalks and large berries (8–14 mm). It grows in bogs from the southern Yukon and NWT to Idaho. **Small bog cranberry** (***Oxycoccus microcarpus***) has smaller leaves (2–6 mm long), hairless flower stalks and smaller berries (5–10 mm). It grows in cold bogs from Alaska to Alberta and northern BC. • All false-wintergreens contain oil of wintergreen (methyl salicylate), which is considered an antirheumatic. These plants have been widely used through the years in remedies for aches and pains. The berries and young leaves have a pleasant wintergreen flavour, but they can be **toxic** in **large quantities**.

Key to Blueberries, Whortleberries & Huckleberries (*Vaccinium* species)

1a. Leaves thick, evergreen, shiny on upper surface ..... ***V. vitis-idaea*** (see *V. scoparium*, p. 79)
1b. Leaves thin, mostly deciduous, not shiny on upper surface 2
  2a. Branches green or yellow-green, strongly angled; plants low (10–20 cm tall) and somewhat matted; berries red to bluish-black 3
    3a. Branches numerous, fine and delicate (broom-like), hairless to slightly hairy; leaves 6–12 mm long; berries bright red .... ***V. scoparium*** (p. 79)
    3b. Branches few, coarse and thick (not broom-like), usually slightly hairy; leaves 10–30 mm long; berries dark red to bluish-black .... ***V. myrtillus*** (see *V. membranaceum*, p. 80)
  2b. Branches brownish or reddish, at most slightly angled; plants taller (often over 30 cm tall); berries blue to blackish 4
    4a. Flowers in clusters of 1–4 in leaf axils; sepals triangular, persistent in fruit; berries blue with a whitish bloom .... ***V. uliginosum*** (see *V. caespitosum*, p. 80)
    4b. Flowers borne singly in leaf axils; sepals rounded, deciduous; berries various 5
      5a. Plants 5–30 cm tall; berries 5–8 mm wide; leaves somewhat saw-toothed above mid-length .... ***V. cespitosum*** (p. 80)
      5b. Plants 30–150 cm tall; berries 8–10 mm wide; leaves toothless or sharply toothed to below mid-length 6
        6a. Leaves 2–5 cm long, finely toothed; berries black to dark purple .... ***V. membranaceum*** (p. 80)
        6b. Leaves 1–3 cm long, usually toothless; berries blue, with a whitish bloom .... ***V. ovalifolium*** (see *V. membranaceum,* p. 80)

GROUSEBERRY; WHORTLEBERRY
Vaccinium scoparium

General: Dwarf, deciduous shrub, **10–20 cm tall**; **branches green, strongly angled**, slender, numerous and erect (**broom-like**), often forming lacy mats.

Leaves: Alternate, ovate, widest near middle, **6–12 mm long**, sharp-pointed, **finely toothed**, thin, bright green.

Flowers: Pinkish, urn-shaped, about 3 mm long, nodding, single from leaf axils; June to July.

Fruits: Bright red (sometimes purplish) **berries, 3–5 mm across**.

Where Found: Open to wooded sites; foothills to subalpine; BC and Alberta to Colorado.

Notes: Lingonberry (***V. vitis-idaea***) (lower photo), also called **mountain cranberry**, is a tiny, mat-forming species more similar to the false-wintergreens and bog cranberries (p. 78) than to the blueberries. It has leathery, evergreen leaves that are glossy green above and pale with dark dots (hairs) beneath. Its berries are bright red and cranberry-like. Lingonberry grows in dry to moist sites from the foothills to alpine zones from Alaska to BC and Alberta. • Lingonberries provide a refreshing, though tart, trail snack, and they make excellent cranberry sauce. • Grouseberry is especially common on the forest floor of coniferous stands, where it forms a lacy groundcover. It could be mistaken for low bilberry (p. 80), which also has green, angled branches, but that species has coarser branches that are not broom-like; its leaves are larger (10–20 mm long), and its berries are purplish to black. • These sweet, red berries are very small, and it could take hours to collect even a small quantity, but some native peoples gathered them using combs. They were usually eaten raw. • If you are looking for grouse, look for this plant. Grouse eat all parts of the shrub—hence the common name 'grouseberry.' Many birds and small mammals eat the berries. • The species name, *scoparium*, from the Latin, *scopula*, 'broom twig,' refers to the broom-like form of these small shrubs.

DWARF BLUEBERRY
Vaccinium cespitosum

General: Spreading, deciduous shrub, 5–30 cm tall; branches **round,** or slightly angled, yellowish to **reddish**, usually fine-hairy; **often forming mats** from widely spreading rhizomes.

Leaves: Alternate, **lance-shaped, widest above middle, wedge-shaped at base**, 1–3 cm long, toothed, thin, **prominently veined** beneath.

Flowers: Whitish to pink, narrowly urn-shaped with 5 small lobes, 4–5 mm long, nodding; single flowers in leaf axils; May to July.

Fruits: Round, **blue berries with a greyish bloom**, 5–8 mm wide.

Where Found: Moist to dry, wooded to open sites; montane to alpine; the Yukon and NWT to Colorado.

Notes: Bog blueberry (***V. uliginosum***) also has rounded, reddish twigs, but its leaves are firmer, toothless and dull green, and its flowers have 4 (rather than 5) lobes and 8 (rather than 10) stamens. Its flowers grow in clusters of 1–4. Bog blueberry grows in bogs and on alpine slopes from Alaska to Alberta and northern BC. • The berries of dwarf blueberry and bog blueberry are juicy and sweet, and they can be eaten fresh or used like commercial blueberries in jams, jellies, syrups, pancakes, muffins and so on. They were widely used by native peoples, either fresh or dried in cakes for later use. These cakes were a popular trade item among some tribes.

BLACK HUCKLEBERRY; MOUNTAIN HUCKLEBERRY
Vaccinium membranaceum

General: Deciduous shrub, erect, **0.3–1.5 m tall**; branches numerous, **yellowish-green and slightly angled** when young.

Leaves: Alternate, ovate to elliptic, **2–5 cm long, thin, finely toothed**, pointed, hairless, bright green in summer, red or purple in autumn.

Flowers: Creamy **pink** to yellowish-pink, **round–urn-shaped**, 5–6 mm long; single flowers on slender stalks from leaf axils; April to June.

Fruits: Black to dark purple berries, 8–10 mm across.

Where Found: Moist, open or wooded sites; foothills to montane; the southern Yukon and NWT to Wyoming.

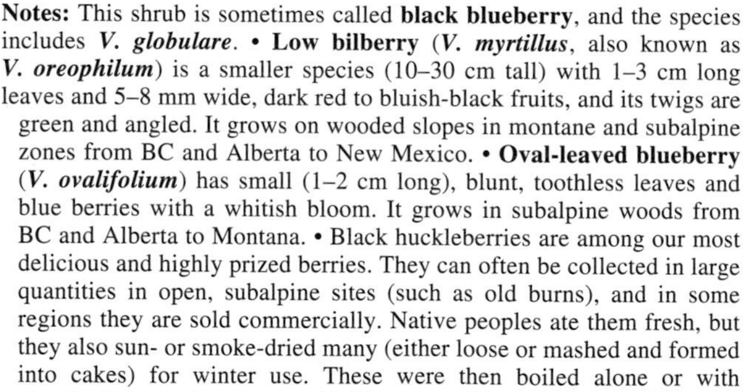

Notes: This shrub is sometimes called **black blueberry**, and the species includes ***V. globulare***. • **Low bilberry** (***V. myrtillus***, also known as ***V. oreophilum***) is a smaller species (10–30 cm tall) with 1–3 cm long leaves and 5–8 mm wide, dark red to bluish-black fruits, and its twigs are green and angled. It grows on wooded slopes in montane and subalpine zones from BC and Alberta to New Mexico. • **Oval-leaved blueberry** (***V. ovalifolium***) has small (1–2 cm long), blunt, toothless leaves and blue berries with a whitish bloom. It grows in subalpine woods from BC and Alberta to Montana. • Black huckleberries are among our most delicious and highly prized berries. They can often be collected in large quantities in open, subalpine sites (such as old burns), and in some regions they are sold commercially. Native peoples ate them fresh, but they also sun- or smoke-dried many (either loose or mashed and formed into cakes) for winter use. These were then boiled alone or with roots. Today, they are eaten fresh, made into jams and jellies, or used in pancakes, muffins, etc. • Roots and stems of black huckleberry were used to make a tea for treating heart trouble, arthritis and rheumatism. • Bears and birds also enjoy these berries. Deer, moose and elk browse on the leaves and twigs.

FALSE-AZALEA
Menziesia ferruginea

General: Deciduous shrub, erect to spreading, 0.5–2 m tall; twigs with fine, **rust-coloured, sticky, glandular** hairs, skunky-smelling when crushed.

Leaves: Alternate, **elliptic, often broadest above middle**, 3–6 cm long, thin, **glandular-hairy, with midvein protruding at tip** and small, rounded teeth on edges, mostly clustered near branch tips, dull, light to blue-green in summer, crimson-orange in winter.

Flowers: Peach-pink to greenish-orange, **urn-shaped**, 6–8 mm long, nodding on long, slender stalks, in clusters at base of new growth; May to July.

Fruits: Dry, **oval capsules**, 5–7 mm long, 4-parted.

Where Found: Moist, wooded sites; foothills to montane; BC and Alberta to Wyoming.

Notes: This species is also known as ***M. glabella***. • When not in flower, this shrub could be mistaken for white-flowered rhododendron (*Rhododendron albiflorum*, below), but rhododendron leaves are glossier, and their midveins do not protrude from their tips. • According to Kunkel (1984), these fruits have been used for food, fresh or dried, but this seems very unlikely. Like most members of the heath family, false-azalea contains the **poison** andromedotoxin. Poisoning and death of sheep, as a result of eating false-azalea, have been reported. • This attractive plant can be propagated from cuttings, but growth from seeds is slow, and it requires 2–3 transplantings before the young shrubs are large enough to plant. Young plants make good bonsai or planter subjects. • This shrub is also known as **fool's huckleberry**, because the leaves resemble those of a huckleberry, but the fruit is a dry capsule rather than a berry.

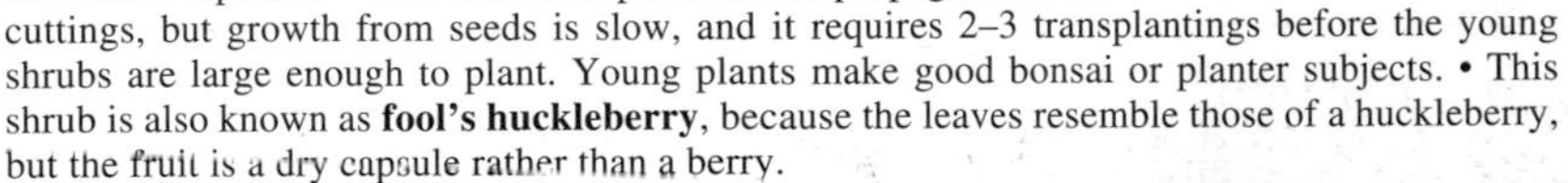

WHITE RHODODENDRON
Rhododendron albiflorum

General: Slender, deciduous shrub, erect to spreading, 50–200 cm tall; small branches with coarse, reddish hairs.

Leaves: Alternate, **crowded near branch tips**, lance-shaped, **widest above middle**, 2–9 cm long, **glossy** above with fine, rusty hairs, green above, paler beneath, bronze to orange in autumn; **midvein not protruding** from tip.

Flowers: Whitish, cup-shaped, 1.5–2 cm across, with 5 broad petals joined at base, on short, glandular, hairy stalks; **nodding in groups of 1–4** from base of this year's growth; June to August.

Fruits: Woody, glandular-hairy, oval capsules, 6–8 mm long.

Where Found: Moist forests; montane to subalpine; BC and Alberta to Montana.

Notes: Lapland rosebay (***R. lapponicum***) (lower photo) is a dwarf (5–25 cm tall), northern species with showy clusters of bright rose-purple flowers. Its leaves are thicker and longer lived (evergreen), and its stems and leaves are covered with dense, rusty-brown scales. Lapland rosebay grows on moist slopes in the alpine zone from Alaska to Alberta and northern BC. • Children have been **poisoned** by eating the leaves and flowers of white rhododendron, and livestock have died from eating these shrubs. • The Thompson lined their berry baskets with white rhododendron branches and also put them over the berries to keep the fruit fresh. The wood was used to make flat spoons for whipping soapberries. • Lapland rosebay always grows on calcium-rich soils, unlike most rhododendrons. Many rhododendrons are grown in gardens, but this species is a true northerner, and it does not survive transplanting to warmer, drier climates.

WILDFLOWERS

This section includes the non-woody flowering plants, with the exceptions of the grasses, sedges, rushes and a few aquatic species. There are 1,000s of different wildflowers in the Rocky Mountains, so only the most distinctive and/or common species could be included in this guide. Wildflowers are the largest group of plants in the guide, with more than 700 species from over 50 families. They are organized by family, and similar species are placed close together for easy comparison. Representatives from a few of the bigger families are illustrated below as a general guide to some of the larger groups.

Flower colour is a striking characteristic that spans many families, so it is rarely used to separate major groups. The following 6 pages provide a general colour key to the wildflowers in this guide. All of the species are not shown, but representatives of the major groups are included. These representatives will guide you to the section of the book where flowers of that type are found.

LILY FAMILY (pp. 90–100)
—leaf veins parallel; flowers radially symmetrical; flower parts in 3s; petals and sepals often similar (tepals).

ORCHID FAMILY (pp. 102–108)
—leaf veins parallel; flowers bilaterally symmetrical, usually with a large lower lip; flower parts in 3s; petals and sepals often similar (tepals).

CARROT FAMILY (pp. 109–115)
—flowers small, in flat-topped, umbrella-shaped clusters; leaves often finely divided and 'fern-like'; fruits dry, seed-like, often ribbed.

PINK FAMILY (pp. 124–129)
—leaves opposite, small and simple; flowers radially symmetrical, usually white or pink, with 5 separate petals and 5 partly fused sepals; capsules usually splitting open by teeth at tip.

SAXIFRAGE FAMILY (pp. 131–136)
—leaves simple, usually alternate or basal; flowers radially symmetrical, with 5 separate petals and 5 sepals; fruits often in pairs with 2 diverging tips.

MUSTARD FAMILY (pp. 137–145)
—flowers with 4 sepals and 4 spreading petals in a cross-like arrangement; fruits pod-like capsules, splitting lengthwise in 2.

ROSE FAMILY (pp. 146–152)
—flowers radially symmetrical, usually with 5 showy petals and 5 sepals alternating smaller bractlets; leaves alternate, usually with stipules at base.

BUTTERCUP FAMILY (pp. 153–164)
—flowers highly variable, radially symmetrical with simple petals (like anemones and buttercups) or spurred petals (like columbines) or bilaterally symmetrical (like delphiniums); fruits dry 'seeds' (achenes) or pods (follicles).

PEA FAMILY (pp. 165–174)
—leaves alternate, with stipules, usually compound; flowers usually bilaterally symmetrical with a lower keel and 2 wing petals (like sweet peas); fruits pods (legumes).

FIGWORT FAMILY (pp. 193–202)
—leaves commonly opposite or whorled; flowers usually bilaterally symmetrical, with a 2-lobed upper lip and a 3-lobed lower lip; fruits egg-shaped to round capsules.

ASTER FAMILY (pp. 215–258)
—flowers in dense, flower-like heads (like asters or dandelions), tiny, with petals fused and strap-like (ray florets) or tubular (disc florets); fruit dry 'seeds' (achenes), often tipped with a tuft of fine bristles.

p. 237 p. 237 p. 239 p. 248 p. 235
p. 114 p. 246 p. 222 p. 149 p. 156
p. 180 p. 158 p. 147 p. 97 p. 98
p. 121 p. 198 p. 200 p. 135 p. 130
p. 177 p. 168 p. 194 p. 200 p. 199
p. 103 p. 117 p. 220 p. 237 p. 221

p. 152 p. 151 p. 181 p. 162 p. 169

p. 168 p. 205 p. 117 p. 172 p. 132

p. 143 p. 212 p. 208 p. 188 p. 147

p. 159 p. 212 p. 98 p. 123 p. 136

p. 209 p. 211 p. 96 p. 99 p. 160

p. 128 p. 127 p. 132 p. 134 p. 176

p. 140 p. 234 p. 111 p. 115 p. 206
p. 167 p. 136 p. 133 p. 95 p. 118
p. 245 p. 234 p. 258 p. 197 p. 116
p. 180 p. 209 p. 196 p. 103 p. 104
p. 108 p. 210 p. 105 p. 100 p. 133
p. 235 p. 226 p. 111 p. 117 p. 95

p. 209 p. 236 p. 214 p. 227 p. 183

p. 129 p. 185 p. 185 p. 164 p. 176

p. 101 p. 93 p. 101 p. 196 p. 166

p. 202 p. 203 p. 204 p. 195 p. 186

p. 203 p. 184 p. 224 p. 187 p. 160

p. 185 p. 190 p. 195 p. 207 p. 192

p. 187 p. 159 p. 208 p. 175 p. 205

p. 253 p. 227 p. 190 p. 170 p. 163

p. 226 p. 122 p. 106 p. 189 p. 179

p. 139 p. 91 p. 228 p. 186 p. 146

p. 178 p. 148 p. 210 p. 211 p. 182

p. 183 p. 197 p. 104 p. 177 p. 188

p. 210 p. 167 p. 92 p. 225 p. 192

p. 213 p. 122 p. 181 p. 169 p. 197

p. 197 p. 106 p. 129 p. 129 p. 173

p. 226 p. 255 p. 152 p. 94 p. 197

p. 130 p. 259 p. 261 p. 194 p. 198

p. 97 p. 220 p. 189 p. 162 p. 97

LILY FAMILY

The lily family (Liliaceae) is a large and varied family of perhaps 2,500 species, with a cosmopolitan distribution. They are mostly perennial herbs, from rhizomes, bulbs or fleshy roots. The **parallel-veined leaves** are all basal, or they may be alternate or whorled on the stem. The radially symmetrical flowers, which often are large and showy, have **flower parts mostly in 3s**, and the **petals and sepals are often very similar** in size, shape and colour. Fruits are 3-chambered capsules or berries.

Key to Lily Family (Liliaceae) Genera

1a. Leaves linear, grass-like 2
  2a. Flowers in umbrella-shaped clusters (umbels) 3
    3a. Plants with onion odour; flowers generally less than 1.5 cm long, pink to purple or white .... ***Allium*** (p. 91)
    3b. Plants lacking onion odour; flowers more than 1.5 cm long, blue ...... ***Triteleia*** (p. 92)
  2b. Flowers solitary or in clusters, but not in umbels 4
    4a. Sepals and petals very different in colour and size: petals yellowish-white, with purple markings at base; sepals green, smaller .... ***Calochortus*** (p. 96)
    4b. Sepals and petals similar in size, and generally in colour 5
      5a. Flowers solitary, white (sometimes with purple veins) .... ***Lloydia*** (see *Clintonia*, p. 98)
      5b. Flowers in clusters 6
        6a. Flowers purplish-blue .... ***Camassia*** (p. 93)
        6b. Flowers white or greenish white (occasionally purplish-green) 7
          7a. Plants robust, 50–150 cm tall, usually on drier sites 8
            8a. Flowers 4–5 cm long; leaves with sharp, rigid points ..... ***Yucca*** (p. 95)
            8b. Flowers about 1 cm long; leaves without sharp, rigid points .... ***Xerophyllum*** (p. 95)
          7b. Plants smaller, 10–70 cm tall, usually on moist to wet sites 9
            9a. Leaves attached sideways to stem (iris-like); growing from rhizomes .... ***Tofieldia*** (p. 93)
            9b. Leaves not attached sideways to stem; growing from bulbs 10
              10a. Stems slender; flowers tubular to bell-shaped, nodding on slender stalks, yellowish-green to purplish-green .... ***Stenanthium*** (p. 94)
              10b. Stems stout; flowers saucer-shaped, fairly erect, not nodding, white to greenish-white .... ***Zigadenus*** (p. 94)

1b. Leaves broader, not grass-like 11
  11a. Petals broad, white; sepals narrower, green .... ***Trillium*** (p. 96)
  11b. Sepals and petals similar in size and (generally) colour 12
    12a. Leaves mostly on flowering stems, gradually smaller upwards 12
      13a. Plants with scaly bulbs; some leaves usually in whorls; tepals at least 1.2 cm long 14
        14a. Tepals less than 3 cm long, yellow to brown .... ***Fritillaria*** (p. 97)
        14b. Tepals 4–10 cm long, orange to brick-red .... ***Lilium*** (p. 97)
      13b. Plants with rhizomes; leaves not in whorls; tepals generally less than 1.2 cm long 15
        15a. Flowers more than 10, in clusters at stem tips 16
          16a. Plants robust, usually over 1 m tall; leaves prominently ribbed; 3 styles; 6 tepals 6–17 mm long ... ***Veratrum*** (p. 100)
          16b. Plants usually less than 1 m tall; leaves not prominently ribbed; 1 style; 4 tepals 2–7 mm long .... ***Maianthemum*** (p. 99)
        15b. Flowers 1–few, along stems or in small clusters at tip 17
          17a. Flowers borne singly, hanging from lower side of stem at each leaf, often hidden by leaves .... ***Streptopus*** (p. 100)
          17b. Flowers 1–3 at branch tips .... ***Disporum*** (p. 99)
    12b. Leaves mostly basal; stem leaves rapidly reduced upwards or absent 18
      18a. Plants with rhizomes; flowers white; blue berries .... ***Clintonia*** (p. 98)
      18b. Plants from corms; flowers yellow, with tepals strongly turned backwards; fruits dry capsules .... ***Erythronium*** (p. 98)

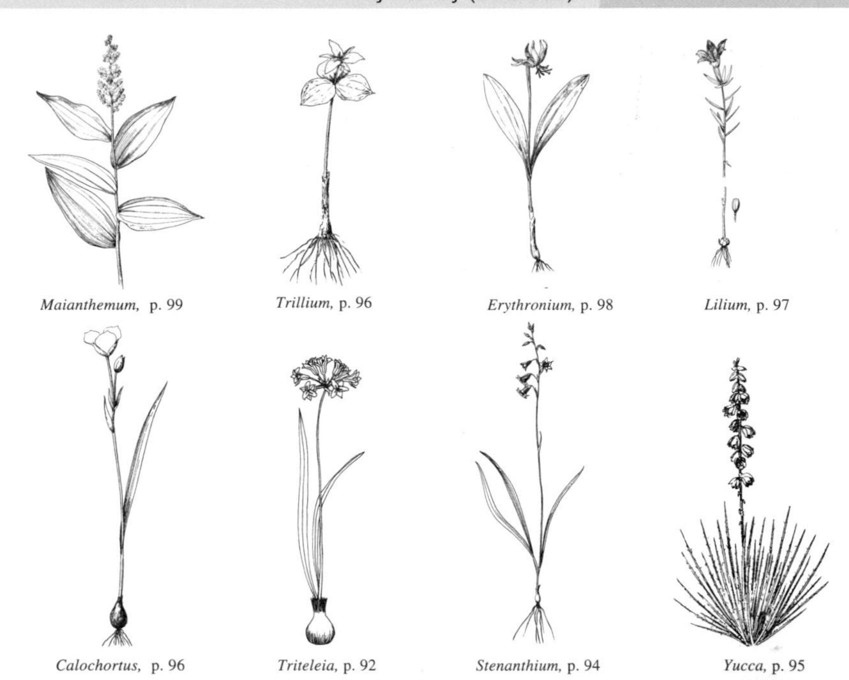

Maianthemum, p. 99 | *Trillium*, p. 96 | *Erythronium*, p. 98 | *Lilium*, p. 97

Calochortus, p. 96 | *Triteleia*, p. 92 | *Stenanthium*, p. 94 | *Yucca*, p. 95

NODDING ONION
Allium cernuum

General: Perennial herb **smelling strongly of onion**; stems slender, leafless, 10–50 cm tall, arched at tip; from **egg-shaped bulbs** on short rhizomes, 1–2 cm thick, usually in clusters, with pinkish to brownish, **membranous outer layers with parallel (not netted) fibres**.

Leaves: Basal, grass-like, 3–7 mm wide, 10–20 cm long, **flat or keeled**, green during flowering.

Flowers: Pink to rose-purple, bell-shaped, 6–7 mm across, with 6 rounded, egg-shaped, 4–6 mm long petals (tepals); few flowers in **nodding, flat-topped clusters** (umbels); June to early August.

Fruits: 3-lobed capsules with 6 points (crests) at tip, about 4 mm long.

Where Found: Moist to dry, open sites; plains to montane; BC and Alberta to New Mexico.

Notes: Short-styled onion (***A. brevistylum***) has smaller (7–15-flowered), erect clusters of larger flowers with pointed, lance-shaped, 10–13 mm long petals (tepals). Also, its stamens and styles are only 1/2 as long as the tepals, so they are not visible without close examination. Short-styled onion grows on wet sites in the montane and subalpine zones from Idaho and Montana to Colorado. • Two common onions have erect flower clusters, and their bulbs are covered with net-like, fibrous layers. **Geyer's onion** (***A. geyeri***) has 3 or more leaves from the base of each stalk, and its flowers are usually deep pink. It is found from the plains to the montane, in wet meadows and along streams from Alberta and BC to New Mexico. • **Prairie onion** (***A. textile***) usually has 2 leaves per stalk and its flowers are white. It is found from the plains to the lower montane in dry, open sites, from Alberta to New Mexico. • Nodding onion is edible, and its bulbs were widely eaten by native peoples and European settlers, either raw, cooked or dried for winter. Cooking removes the strong smell and flavour, converting the sugar 'inulin' to the more digestible 'fructose,' and the bulbs become very sweet. • Wild onions (*Allium* spp.) resemble, and often grow in the same habitats as, **mountain death-camas** (p. 94), which is **poisonous**. Mountain death-camas does **not** smell like an onion. Do **not** try the 'taste test.'

WILD CHIVES
Allium schoenoprasum

General: Onion-smelling, perennial herb; stems round, 20–60 cm tall; from **bulbs up to 10 mm thick** with membranous outer layers.

Leaves: Alternate, usually 2, **cylindrical, hollow, sheathing** the stem, 1–7 mm wide.

Flowers: Rose-pink to purplish (sometimes white), 8–14 mm long, tubular–bell-shaped, with 6 lance-shaped petals (tepals) spreading slightly at tips, short-stalked; in erect, **dense heads 2–5 cm across**; April to August.

Fruits: Egg-shaped, 3-lobed capsules with 3–6 black, honey-combed seeds.

Where Found: Moist to wet, open sites; plains to montane; Alaska to Colorado.

Notes: This species has also been called ***A. sibiricum***. • These plants can be used like domestic chives, for flavouring salads, vegetables and meat dishes. Some people find them strong by themselves, but others pickle them or use them as a cooked vegetable, served hot with butter. • Care must be taken not to confuse wild chives with its **poisonous** relative, **mountain death-camas** (p. 94), which has no onion-like smell. Never eat an onion that doesn't smell like an onion. • The most common medicinal use of chives in the past has been in treating coughs and colds. The juice was either boiled down to a thick syrup or a sliced bulb was placed in sugar; the resulting syrup was taken. Dried chive bulbs were burned in smudges to fumigate the patient, or they were ground and inhaled like snuff to clear the sinuses. Wild chives were also said to stimulate appetite and aid digestion, though water in which they had been crushed and soaked for 12 hours was swallowed on an empty stomach to rid the system of worms. The juice is somewhat antiseptic, and it was used by native peoples and sourdoughs to moisten sphagnum moss for use as a dressing on wounds and sores. Crushed bulbs were also used to treat insect bites and stings, hives, burns, scalds, sores, blemishes and even snakebites. • The flowering stems dry well, and they make a beautiful addition to dried flower arrangements.

WHITE HYACINTH; GOPHERNUTS
Triteleia grandiflora

General: Perennial herb; stems 20–60 cm tall; from **deep, scaly, bulbous stem bases** (corms) about 2 cm thick.

Leaves: Basal, linear, 1–2, 25–50 cm long, flat but **keeled beneath**.

Flowers: Deep to light blue, about 2 cm long and wide, **bell-shaped,** with 6 flaring petals (tepals); **3 inner tepals with ruffled edges**; anthers blue, 2–3 mm long; several flowers in **open, flat-topped clusters** (umbels); April to July.

Fruits: Rounded capsules, 6–10 mm long.

Where Found: Dry, open or wooded slopes; plains to montane; southern BC to Wyoming.

Notes: This species has also been called ***Brodiaea douglasii***. • White hyacinth bulbs were collected for food and medicine by the Thompson tribes. They were dug in spring (along with the bulbs of yellowbells [p. 97]), just before the shoots appeared above ground. They were said to be similar to the bulbs of nodding onion (p. 91), and they were used accordingly. • In 1 myth, white hyacinth bulbs saved a family from starvation. They were believed to have some magical powers, and they were included in medicine bags to increase the potency of the bag. • The species name *douglasii* commemorates David Douglas, a Scottish botanist who collected plants in North America for the Royal Horticultural Society of England in the 1800s.

COMMON CAMAS
Camassia quamash

General: Perennial herb; stems 20–60 cm tall; from **egg-shaped bulbs** 1–3 cm thick.

Leaves: Basal, grass-like, linear, 6–15 mm wide, 20–40 cm long.

Flowers: Pale to deep blue or violet, star-shaped, about 4–5 cm across, with **6 linear, 3–9-nerved petals** (tepals); many flowers in elongating clusters 5–30 cm long; May to June.

Fruits: Egg-shaped capsules, 12–15 mm long.

Where Found: Moist meadows; plains to foothills; BC and Alberta to Wyoming.

Notes: Camas provided one of the most prized root crops, and many tribes fought for the right to collect in certain meadows. Its role was likened to that of cereal plants in 'civilized' life in Europe. Settlers and explorers used it less, because large quantities caused **vomiting** and **diarrhea** in the uninitiated and, as Father Nicholas Point pointed out, 'very disagreeable effects for those who do not like strong odors or the sound that accompanies them.' • Girls competed in the annual camas harvest to show their worth as future wives. One young woman was reported to have collected and prepared 60, 42 *l* sacks of camas roots. Men were excluded from the harvest, because they would bring 'bad luck,' and if a woman burned any bulbs, it was said that some of her relatives would soon die. The roots were roasted, pounded, made into cakes, eaten raw, or stone boiled, but most were cooked and dried. The bulbs were baked in pits with hot stones for several days, and when they were done, they were dark brown, with a glue-like consistency and a sweet taste, like that of molasses. They were then mashed together and made into cakes that were sun-dried for storage. During the cooking process insulin (an indigestible sugar) breaks down to fructose; cooked, dried bulbs are 43 percent fructose by weight. Camas was the principal sweetening agent for many tribes prior to the introduction of sugar. Cooked, dried bulbs kept indefinitely. David Thompson reported eating 36-year-old bulbs that still had good flavour, though they had lost their aroma after 2 years. • Deer and elk eat camas in early spring.

STICKY FALSE-ASPHODEL
Tofieldia glutinosa

General: Glandular, sticky, perennial herb; stems **tufted**, erect, 10–50 cm tall; from short rhizomes and fibrous roots.

Leaves: Alternate, on lower stem, linear, **iris-like**, 5–15 cm long.

Flowers: White or greenish-tinged, star-shaped, about 7–9 mm across with 6 oblong petals (tepals), often with conspicuous, purplish anthers; several flowers in 3s, forming **dense, elongating heads** (racemes) **2–5 cm long**; June to August.

Fruits: Erect capsules, 3-pointed, egg-shaped, about 5–6 mm long, **yellowish or red**.

Where Found: Wet to moist, open sites, including meadows, bogs and fens; montane to alpine; the Yukon and NWT to Wyoming.

Notes: Dwarf false-asphodel (***T. pusilla***) (lower photo) is a smaller (5–20 cm tall), hairless species with pale green, leafless stems and small (0.5–3 cm long) flower clusters. It grows on wet, calcium-rich sites in subalpine and alpine zones from Alaska to Montana. • Northern natives boiled or baked these edible rhizomes. • The genus name *Tofieldia* commemorates the English botanist Thomas Tofield (1730–79). The species name *glutinosa* is from the Latin *gluten*, 'glue,' in reference to the sticky stems and flower stalks of this species; *pusillus* means 'small.' The origin of the common name 'false asphodel' is less clear. Homer named asphodel as the flower of the Elysian Fields—*And rest at last, where sould unbodied dwell/ In ever-flow'ring meads of asphodel* (*The Odyssey*: xxiv.1.19 of Pope's translation). This explanation would fit with 1 possible origin—the Greek *a*, 'not,' and *spodos*, 'ashes.' Another source says that it is from the Greek *a*, 'not,' and *sphallo*, 'I surpass,' to indicate a stately plant of unsurpassed beauty. In medieval England, this name was somehow corrupted to the now widely used 'daffodil' (*Narcissus* spp.).

MOUNTAIN DEATH-CAMAS
Zigadenus elegans

General: Grey-green, perennial herb, often with a whitish waxy coating (bloom); stems erect, 15–70 cm tall, often pinkish; from **oval bulbs covered with blackish scales**.

Leaves: Mainly **basal, grass-like**, keeled, 8–30 cm long, 2–15 mm wide; stem leaves few and small.

Flowers: Greenish-white to yellowish-white with 6 dark green, heart-shaped glands near centre (1 at the base of each petal [tepal]), saucer-shaped, about 2 cm across, foul-smelling; 3–several flowers in long, open clusters (racemes), sometimes branched and panicle-like; June to August.

Fruits: Erect, 3-lobed capsules, 15–20 mm long, egg-shaped to oblong.

Where Found: Moist, open sites; foothills to alpine; Alaska to New Mexico.

Notes: The genus name is sometimes spelled ***Zygadenus***. • **Meadow death-camas** (***Z. venenosus***, including ***Z. gramineus***) is similar to mountain death-camas, but it has smaller flowers (about 1–1.5 cm across) with oblong to round (not heart-shaped) glands, and its petals are attached at the base of the ovary (rather than to 1/3 of the way up). Meadow death-camas grows in open areas at low elevations from southern BC and Alberta to Utah and Colorado. • All parts of both species contain the **poisonous** alkaloid zygadenine, which some claim to be more potent than strychnine. Two bulbs, raw or cooked, can be fatal. If someone has eaten this plant, induce vomiting and get medical help. Poisonings result from confusing these bulbs with those of edible species such as wild onions (p. 91), camas (p. 93), white hyacinth (p. 92), mariposa-lilies (p. 96) or fritillarias (p. 97). Onions are easily identified by their distinctive smell, but other bulbs can be difficult to distinguish once the distinctive flowers have faded. If there is any doubt, do not eat it! • The genus name *Zigadenus* was derived from the Greek *zygon,* 'a yoke,' in reference to the paired (yoked) glands at the base of each petal. The species name *elegans* means 'elegant,' which this plant certainly is.

Z. venenosus

BRONZEBELLS; MOUNTAINBELLS
Stenanthium occidentale

General: Perennial herb; stems **erect, 20–40 cm tall**; from 2–4 cm long, **oval bulbs**.

Leaves: Basal, 2–3, narrowly lance-shaped, 15–30 cm long, 3–25 mm wide.

Flowers: Bronze to purplish-green, tubular–bell-shaped, 8–15 mm long with 6 flaring, back-curled petals (tepals); 3–25 **hanging** in elongated, sometimes branched clusters (racemes); June to August.

Fruits: Slender, membranous, 3-beaked capsules, to about 2 cm long.

Where Found: Wet to moist, open or wooded sites; montane to alpine; BC and Alberta to Idaho and Montana.

Notes: These plants are **poisonous**, and they should never be taken internally. Some natives reported that bronzebells was a useful medicine, but that you had to be an expert to use it. • This plant was sometimes called 'bleed-nose-plant,' because it was said that you would get a nosebleed if you touched it. • The genus name *Stenanthium* was derived from the Greek *stenos*, 'narrow,' and *anthos*, 'flower,' in reference to the narrowly bell-shaped flowers. The species name *occidentale* means 'of the west.'

BEARGRASS
Xerophyllum tenax

General: Robust, evergreen, perennial herb; flowering stems **erect, 50–150 cm tall**; from stout, short rhizomes.

Leaves: Mainly **basal in large clumps, tough, wiry, grass-like, 20–60 cm long**, 2–4 mm wide, with sharp, finely toothed edges; stem leaves alternate, similar to basal leaves but smaller.

Flowers: White, star-like, with 6 spreading petals (tepals), about 1.5 cm across, long-stalked, fragrant; many flowers in **showy, club-shaped, elongating, 'bottle-brush' clusters** (racemes), mature from bottom to top; May to August.

Fruits: Dry, oval, 3-lobed capsules, 5–7 mm long, few-seeded.

Where Found: Dry, open sites, occasionally in forests; montane to subalpine; southeastern BC and southwestern Alberta to Idaho and Montana.

Notes: This name is sometimes spelled ***Zerophyllum***. • The leafy flowering stems die after flowering. Most plants flower every 3–10 years, and often all of the plants in a population will bloom together, covering a slope with white and filling the air with their perfume. • Some tribes used the tough, slender leaves to weave hats, baskets and capes. • These plants are difficult to grow and they do not do well in gardens. They are best left in their natural habitat. • The flowers and young seed pods are eaten by rodents and large mammals such as elk and bighorn sheep. Mountain goats often eat the leaves during winter, but these tough tussocks are unpalatable to other animals. Bears eat the fleshy leaf sheaths in spring—hence the common name 'beargrass.'

NARROW-LEAVED YUCCA
Yucca glauca

General: Coarse, evergreen, perennial herb; stems erect, 50–150 cm tall; from short, woody root crowns.

Leaves: Basal, densely tufted, stiff, linear, sharp-pointed, 20–60 cm long; edges inrolled, whitish, with few frayed fibres.

Flowers: Creamy white to greenish-white, showy, bell-shaped, 4–5 cm long and wide, with 6 leathery, egg-shaped petals (tepals); many flowers **nodding in long clusters** (racemes); May to July.

Fruits: Hardened, oblong capsules, 5–7 cm long, with many black seeds.

Where Found: Dry, open sites; plains to foothills; southern Alberta to New Mexico.

Notes: The flower petals were eaten raw in salads and the young seed pods were roasted in ashes and eaten. Ripe fruits were split in 1/2 to scrape out their seeds and fibre and the remaining pulp was then baked and eaten. The leaves are also said to have been boiled and eaten, but they are extremely fibrous. • The leaves were split and used as all-purpose ties, but they were not twisted or plaited to make cord or rope. • The Navajo pounded the roots with rocks to remove bark and soften them and then vigorously stirred the softened mass of fibres in warm water to whip up suds. This substance was used as soap to wash wool, clothing, hair and body. It was also said to reduce dandruff and baldness. • Tea made from the roots was thought to clean the sticky covering from an over-sized baby and speed delivery. • Narrow-leaved yucca and a small, white, night-flying moth (the yucca moth, *Pronuba*) depend on one another for survival. These flowers open fully only at night, when they are visited by a female yucca moth. She takes a ball of pollen and flies to another flower, where she eats through the ovary wall and deposits an egg inside. She then climbs to the stigma, deposits the pollen from the first flower, and moves to the anthers to collect a second ball of pollen before flying to the next plant. By fertilizing the flowers, she assures the development of seeds, which will provide food for her young when the eggs hatch, and new plants for future generations of moths. Ripe yucca pods almost always have a tiny hole, where the grub ate its way out.

THREE-SPOT MARIPOSA-LILY
Calochortus apiculatus

General: Perennial herb; stems erect, 10–30 cm tall; from deeply buried, fleshy, **egg-shaped, onion-like bulbs**.

Leaves: Basal, single, flat, **grass-like**, 10–30 cm long, 0.5–1.5 cm wide, usually shorter than stem.

Flowers: Yellowish-white (sometimes with purplish lines) **with 3 dark purple dots (glands) near centre**, broadly cupped, about 3–4 cm across, erect or spreading**; 3 broad petals,** abruptly pointed at tip, hairy on lower $^{1}/_{2}$ and fringed along edges; sepals green, shorter than petals; 1–5 in open clusters (like umbels); late June to early August.

Fruits: Nodding, elliptic, **3-winged capsules**, about 2.5–3 cm long.

Where Found: Dry, open or partly shaded sites; foothills to montane; southern BC and Alberta to Idaho and Montana.

Notes: Elegant mariposa-lily (*C. elegans*) is very similar to three-spot mariposa-lily, but the purple gland at the base of each petal is crescent-shaped, and it is much larger. Elegant mariposa-lily grows on shaded hillsides in foothills and montane zones from Washington to Montana. • Several mariposa lilies have channelled leaves and erect capsules that are triangular in cross-section, rather than winged. **Gunnison's mariposa-lily** (*C. gunnisonii*) has white, pinkish or lavender flowers. It is identified by the broad, purple band and gland-tipped hairs above the gland at the base of each petal. It grows in foothills and montane meadows from Idaho and Montana to New Mexico. • **Sego-lily** (*C. nuttallii*), also known as **Nuttall's mariposa-lily**, has ivory-white flowers with a large, dark spot (gland) as the base of each petal, below a broad, crescent-shaped, reddish-brown or purple band. Sego-lily grows in dry sites in foothills to montane zones from Idaho and Montana to New Mexico. • The bulbs of mariposa-lilies are said to be sweet and nutritious, raw or cooked. They were eaten by many tribes, and were widely used by settlers in Utah when food was scarce.

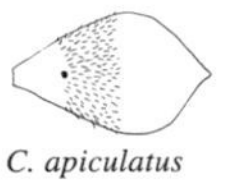

C. apiculatus

C. elegans

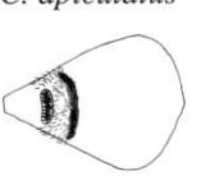

C. gunnisonii

C. nuttallii

WESTERN TRILLIUM; WESTERN WAKEROBIN
Trillium ovatum

General: Perennial herb; stems erect, 10–40 cm tall; from stout, short rhizomes.

Leaves: In a whorl of 3 (sometimes 4–5) **at the stem tip, broadly egg-shaped**, 5–15 cm long, 4–8 cm wide, stalkless.

Flowers: White (pink to purplish with age), with **3 broad, white petals alternating with 3 small, green sepals, about 6–9 cm across**; single, erect, on a 4–5 cm long stalk from the centre of the leaf whorl; March to July.

Fruits: Yellowish-green, berry-like capsules, oval, narrowly winged; seeds numerous, shed in a sticky mass.

Where Found: Moist to wet, shady sites; foothills to subalpine; BC and southwestern Alberta to Colorado.

Notes: Some tribes used the thick rhizomes to help mothers during childbirth—hence the common name '**birthroot**.' The leaves have been used as cooked greens. • Trillium seeds each have a small, oil-rich body that attracts ants. The ants carry the seeds to their nests, where they eat the oil-rich part or feed it to their young, and discard the rest. This is a very effective way to disperse seeds, and North American forests contain many 'ant plants' (plants whose seeds contain oil bodies), including wild ginger (p. 177) and many violets (p. 176) as well as trilliums. • The genus name *Trillium*, from the Latin *tri*, 'three,' refers to the 3 leaves, 3 petals, 3 sepals and 3 stigmas of these plants. The flowers bloom in spring, just as the robins return, or 'wake up,' from their winter absence—hence the name '**wakerobin**.'

YELLOWBELLS
Fritillaria pudica

General: Perennial herb; stems 10–30 cm tall; from **small, scaly, bulb-like corms**.

Leaves: Nearly opposite to whorled, **usually 2, linear**, 3–10 cm long, rather **fleshy**.

Flowers: Yellow, often with purple to orange marks near base, fading orange to brown, **narrowly bell-shaped**, about **1–2 cm long**, with 6 lance-shaped petals (tepals), **nodding; solitary** (sometimes 2–3); April to May.

Fruits: Erect, egg-shaped capsules 2–4 cm long.

Where Found: Moderately dry, open or wooded, grassy sites; plains to montane; southern BC and Alberta to Colorado.

Notes: Purple fritillary (***F. atropurpurea***), also called **leopard lily**, has 1–4 nodding, brown flowers with yellow or white blotches. It has 5–22 narrow (2–7 mm wide), scattered leaves. Purple fritillary grows on grassy slopes in the plains, foothills and montane zones from southern Idaho to New Mexico. • The bulb-like corms, which grow 5–15 cm below ground, produce tiny offsets that are the size of rice grains. Both bulbs and offsets are edible, either raw or cooked. Several tribes gathered these roots in early May and boiled them alone or with bitterroot (p. 122), which was collected at the same time. This use is now discouraged because yellowbells are easily exterminated by heavy harvesting. The fruiting pods are also edible, boiled as a wild green, but they were not used by most tribes. • Bears, gophers and ground squirrels also enjoy eating the corms of yellowbells, and deer and other ungulates feed on the leaves. • Purple fritillary has an odour that most people find very unpleasant, but it is strongly attractive to flies, which probably pollinate these flowers.

WOOD LILY
Lilium philadelphicum

General: Hairless, perennial herb; stems single, erect, 30–60 cm tall; from **whitish, scaly bulbs**.

Leaves: Alternate near stem base, **whorled (usually in 6s) on upper stem, linear** to narrowly lance-shaped, 5–10 cm long.

Flowers: Orange to brick-red, lighter and purplish-dotted in throat, about 8 cm across, goblet-shaped with 6 separate petals (tepals), **erect;** anthers purple; **solitary** (sometimes 2–3) at stem tips; June to July.

Fruits: Erect, cylindrical capsules, broadest above middle, 2–4 cm long.

Where Found: Moist, open to wooded sites; plains to montane; BC and Alberta to New Mexico.

Notes: This species has also been called ***L. umbellatum***. • **Tiger lily** (***L. columbianum***, also known as **Columbia lily**) (lower photo) has smaller flowers (about 3–4 cm across) with petals that curl back towards the base. These beautiful, orange, purple-spotted blooms hang in showy clusters (racemes) of 2–20 at the tips or tall stems (60–120 cm). Tiger lily grows in open or wooded sites in foothills, montane and subalpine zones from BC to Idaho. • When these flowers are picked or mowed, all of the leaves are removed with the stalk, and the plant dies. Digging, mowing, and over-picking have resulted in the near extinction of this beautiful wildflower in populated areas. • The flowers, seeds and bulbs have all been used as food. The bulbs have a strong, bitter, peppery flavour. They were usually cooked and eaten with other foods, but some tribes ate them fresh or dried them for winter storage. • Northern natives used wood lily roots to make medicinal tea that was taken to treat stomach disorders, coughs, tuberculosis and fevers, and that was applied externally to swellings, bruises, wounds and sores. • The wood lily is the floral emblem of Saskatchewan.

YELLOW GLACIER-LILY; SNOW-LILY
Erythronium grandiflorum

General: Perennial herb; stems 10–40 cm tall, leafless, unbranched; from deep, elongated, **bulb-like corms**, frequently forming large patches.

Leaves: Basal, 1 pair, bright green, lance-shaped to elliptic, 10–20 cm long.

Flowers: Bright yellow, nodding, 3–6 cm across, with 6 petals (tepals) curved upwards and 6 large stamens projecting downwards; **solitary** (sometimes 2–3); April to August, depending on elevation.

Fruits: Erect, 3-sided, club-shaped capsules, 3–4 cm long.

Where Found: Moist, rich, shaded to open sites; montane to alpine; BC and Alberta to Colorado and Utah.

Notes: These corms were an important food for some tribes, and dried bulbs were a popular trade item. They are edible raw, but like onions, they are made sweeter and more easily digestible by cooking. Drying also helps this process. The corms sometimes cause a burning sensation, and too many can cause **vomiting**. The leaves are also edible raw or cooked and the fresh, green seed pods are said to taste like string beans when cooked, but most tribes used only the corms. • Removing the bulb kills the plant, and yellow glacier-lily populations have been greatly reduced in some areas by harvesting. These beautiful wildflowers should not be collected. • Black bears, grizzly bears and rodents eat yellow glacier-lily roots, and the seed pods are grazed by deer, elk, sheep and probably goats. • This beautiful mountain lily has also been called **dogtooth violet**, **adder's tongue**, **avalanche lily**, **fawn lily** and **trout lily**.

CORN-LILY; QUEEN'S CUP
Clintonia uniflora

General: Sparsely long-hairy, perennial herb; **stems** erect, 6–15 cm tall, **shorter than leaves, leafless, hairy**; from slender, spreading rhizomes and fibrous roots.

Leaves: Basal, 2–4, lance-shaped to elliptic, 7–20 cm long, 3–5 cm wide, **slightly fleshy and glossy**, hairy on edges.

Flowers: White, about 2–2.5 cm across, **star-like**, with 6 narrow petals (tepals) and 6 large, yellow anthers; **solitary** (sometimes 2); late May to July.

Fruits: Single, **bright metallic-blue berries**, 8–10 mm across, 6–10-seeded.

Where Found: Moist to wet, open to shaded sites; montane to subalpine; BC and Alberta to Idaho and Montana.

Notes: Alplily (***Lloydia serotina***) (lower photo) is also a small lily (5–15 cm tall) with single, whitish, broadly bell-shaped flowers, but it has very narrow (1–2 mm wide), grass-like leaves, and its blooms are small (about 12–15 mm across) and inconspicuous. Alplily is an arctic plant that grows on rocky alpine slopes in the Rocky Mountains from Alaska through BC to New Mexico. • The blue, berry-like fruits were mashed and used as a dye or stain, but many berries were needed to produce good colour. They are considered unpalatable by human standards, but grouse seem to enjoy them. • The genus name *Clintonia* commemorates DeWitt Clinton (1769–1828), a New York politician (as mayor, state senator and eventually governor) who also wrote books about natural history. • The species name *uniflora*, from the Latin *unus,* 'one,' and *floris,* 'flower,' means '1-flowered.'

STAR-FLOWERED FALSE SOLOMON'S-SEAL
Maianthemum stellatum

General: Perennial herb; stems erect, **slightly arching**, 15–60 cm tall, unbranched, finely hairy; from slender, spreading rhizomes.

Leaves: Alternate, lance-shaped, 3–12 cm long, 1–5 cm wide, upper leaves only slightly smaller, flat (sometimes folded down centre), **hairless** and straight on edges.

Flowers: White, star-like with 6 petals (tepals), about 1 cm across; 5–10 in loose, unbranched, 1.5–6 cm long clusters (racemes); May to July.

Fruits: Dark blue or reddish-black berries, 6–10 mm across; immature berries greenish-yellow with 3 or 6 red to purple stripes.

Where Found: Moist (sometimes dry), shaded to open sites; foothills to subalpine; the central Yukon and NWT to Colorado.

Notes: This species is commonly called ***Smilacina stellata***. • Star-flowered false Solomon's-seal could be confused with clasping-leaved twisted-stalk (p. 100) and fairybells (below). The differences between these plants are described in the notes for fairybells. • **False Solomon's-seal (*M. racemosum*,** commonly known as ***S. racemosa***) is easily recognized by its large (5–15 cm long), puffy, pyramidal flower clusters (panicles) and its broader leaves, which have wavy (rather than straight) edges. It grows in moist sites in foothills and montane zones from BC and Alberta to Colorado. • **Three-leaved false Solomon's-seal** (***M. trifolium***, commonly known as ***S. trifolia***) is a small, slender plant with only 3 leaves, and its simple flower clusters are borne on long stalks. It grows in wet woods and bogs from the Yukon and NWT to BC and Alberta. • Solomon's-seal berries are said to be edible, cooked or raw, but they are not sweet, and too many will cause **diarrhea**. The young leaves and shoots have also been eaten, cooked like asparagus or used as a potherb. Young plants resemble shoots of Indian hellebore (p. 100), which is **extremely poisonous**.

M. racemosum

ROUGH-FRUITED FAIRYBELLS
Disporum trachycarpum

General: Perennial herb; stems **leafy**, 30–60 cm tall, with **few branches**; from thick, spreading rhizomes.

Leaves: Alternate, **egg- to lance-shaped**, 3–9 cm long, pointed at tips, rounded to heart-shaped at base, **fringed** with short, spreading hairs, **clasping**.

Flowers: Creamy to greenish-**white**, narrowly **bell-shaped**, 10–15 mm long, nodding; **1–3 at branch tips**; April to July.

Fruits: 1–3 lumpy berries, 8–10 mm across, **bright orange-yellow to scarlet, velvet-warty skinned**, 4–18-seeded.

Where Found: Rich, moist sites; plains to subalpine; BC and Alberta to New Mexico.

Notes: Fairybells could be confused with **clasping-leaved twisted-stalk** (p. 100) and **false Solomon's-seal** (above), but the flowers of clasping leaved twisted-stalk hang from the base of its leaves (not at the stem tips), and false Solomon's-seal has unbranched stems tipped with large clusters of flowers. • **Hooker's fairybells** (***D. hookeri***, also called ***D. oreganum***) is very similar to rough-fruited fairybells, but the hairs on its leaf edges point towards the tip, and its berries are smooth-skinned (not warty), though sometimes hairy. Hooker's fairybells grows in moist, shaded woods at low elevations, from central BC and southwestern Alberta to Oregon and Montana. • These berries are edible, but they have little flavour. Some native peoples considered them poisonous or associated them with ghosts and snakes, possibly because of their brilliant colour and unusual texture. Other tribes ate them occasionally. • Rodents and grouse feed on these berries.

CLASPING-LEAVED TWISTED-STALK
Streptopus amplexifolius

General: Perennial herb; stems erect, 30–100 cm tall, hairless, **branched**, often bent at each leaf (**zigzag**); from short, thick rhizomes with fibrous roots.

Leaves: Alternate, oval to oval–lance-shaped, 5–15 cm long, 2–6 cm wide, **clasping**; undersides grey-green.

Flowers: Greenish-white to **white, bell-shaped,** 8–12 mm long, with 6 flaring to backward-curling petals (tepals); 1 (sometimes 2) **hanging from lower side of each leaf on a thin, kinked stalk**; May to August.

Fruits: Bright red (sometimes to dark purple) when mature, **oval-oblong berries**, about 1 cm long.

Where Found: Moist, rich sites; the Yukon and NWT to New Mexico.

Notes: The flowers and fruits are hidden by the leaves, and they are easily overlooked. • Twisted-stalk could be confused with false Solomon's-seal (p. 99) and fairybells (p. 99). The differences between these plants are described in the notes for fairybells. • Most native peoples regarded clasping-leaved twisted-stalk as poisonous, but some groups ate the young plants and berries, raw or cooked, in soups and stews. Young plants resemble shoots of Indian hellebore (below), which is **extremely poisonous.** • The genus name *Streptopus* was derived from the Greek *streptos*, 'twisted,' and *podos,* 'foot,' in reference to the bent and twisted stalks of the flowers and fruits. The species name *amplexifolius* was derived from the Latin *amplexor*, 'to surround,' and *folius,* 'leaf,' in reference to the clasping leaves of this species.

INDIAN HELLEBORE; GREEN FALSE-HELLEBORE
Veratrum viride

General: Robust, perennial herb; stems erect, 70–200 cm tall, **leafy, hairy, unbranched**, often clustered; from stout, erect rhizomes.

Leaves: Alternate, elliptic, 10–25 cm long, 4–10 cm wide, **clasping, prominently ribbed** (accordion-pleated); upper leaves smaller.

Flowers: Yellow-green to deep **green** with dark green centres, star-shaped, about 2 cm across, musky-smelling; many flowers in 30–70 cm long, **densely flowered, open clusters** (panicles) with spreading to hanging, **tassel-like branches**; June to September.

Fruits: Straw-coloured to dark brown capsules, ovoid, 2–3 cm long; seeds papery, broadly winged.

Where Found: Moist to wet, open or partly shaded sites, often in areas with late snow melt; montane to alpine; the Yukon and NWT to Idaho and Montana.

Notes: This species has also been called ***V. eschscholtzii***. • **California false-hellebore** (***V. californicum***), also known as corn-lily, has larger (about 3 cm across), white to greenish-white flowers in clusters with spreading to ascending (not hanging) branches. It grows in similar, moist habitats in foothills, montane and subalpine zones from Montana to New Mexico. • Both of these species are commonly called **corn-lily**. • False-hellebores are **violently poisonous**. They contain the alkaloid protoveratrine, which slows heartbeat and breathing. **Eating even small amounts can result in unconsciousness, followed by death**. Symptoms include frothing at the mouth, blurred vision, 'lock jaw,' vomiting and diarrhea. People have reported stomach cramps after drinking water in which this plant was growing. Some *Veratrum* species are powdered to make the garden insecticide 'hellebore.' • Indian hellebore was highly respected by many native peoples as a powerful medicine. Native peoples from east of the mountains often travelled great distances to trade for this root. The Flathead, Kutenai and others used the powdered root like snuff to clear the nasal passages. The roots were boiled to make a wash to kill lice. • The genus name *Veratrum* was derived from the Latin *verus*, 'true,' and *atra*, 'black,' because of the black roots. The species name *viride* means 'green,' a reference to the green flowers.

MOUNTAIN BLUE-EYED-GRASS; COMMON BLUE-EYED-GRASS
Sisyrinchium montanum

General: Tufted, perennial herb; **stems several, stiff**, erect, 10–50 cm tall, **flattened and winged**; from short rhizomes and fibrous roots.

Leaves: Basal, linear, **grass-like**, 1–3.5 mm wide.

Flowers: Bluish-purple with a yellow 'eye,' about 1 cm across, star-shaped with 6 egg-shaped, **abruptly pointed petals** (tepals); 1–few flowers, from between 2 unequal, leaf-like bracts, on **stalks longer than lower bract**; April to July.

Fruits: Round capsules, 3–6 mm long.

Where Found: Moist to moderately dry, open sites; plains to subalpine; the southern Yukon and NWT to Colorado.

Notes: *S. montanum* is found across North America. Western plants were often called ***S. angustifolium*** in earlier floras, but that name now applies to an eastern species. A few other species of blue-eyed-grass are found in the Rocky Mountains, but there is a great deal of confusion regarding the taxonomic treatment of this group. Mountain blue-eyed-grass is by far the most common and widespread. • Native peoples used the roots of mountain blue-eyed-grass to make a tea for treating diarrhea, especially in children. A tea made from the entire plant was taken to cure stomachaches and to expel intestinal worms. Herbalists used these teas to treat menstrual disorders and for birth control. Several species have also been used as laxatives. • The common name 'blue-eyed-grass' is apt for these plants. The delicate, blue flowers with their yellow centres look like little eyes peeking out from their grass-like leaves.

WESTERN BLUE FLAG
Iris missouriensis

General: Perennial herb; stems **clumped, about 20–50 cm tall**; from **thick, spreading rhizomes.**

Leaves: Mainly basal, linear, **sword-shaped**, 20–40 cm long, 5–10 mm wide.

Flowers: Pale to deep blue, sometimes pale with purple lines, about **6–7 cm across; 3 backward-curved, purple-lined sepals; 3 erect, narrower and paler petals; 3 flattened, petal-like branches of the style**; 2–4 on leafless stalks; May to early July.

Fruits: Capsules, 3–5 cm long.

Where Found: Moist to wet sites (at least in spring); plains to montane; BC and Alberta to New Mexico.

Notes: Blue flag roots are **poisonous**, and they should never be taken internally. When gathering edible rootstocks such as those of cattails (p. 264) in wetlands, **care must be taken not to confuse them** with blue flag rhizomes. *Iris* rootstocks are odourless and unpleasant-tasting, whereas the rootstocks of cattails are odourless and bland. • Historically, small amounts of blueflag roots were taken to induce vomiting, and blue flag was also thought to stimulate the production of pancreatic enzymes, bile, saliva, urine and sweat, thereby cleansing the system. Until 1947 'blue flag' was an official drug in the US *National Formulary* for the treatment of syphilis, as an alternative to the use of bismuth, arsenic, mercury and so on, but its effectiveness is questionable. Blue flag is more potent than the official medicinal species, and in the past it was harvested for extraction. The fresh roots are said to be effective in treating staph sores, when applied as a poultice.

ORCHID FAMILY (ORCHIDACEAE)

The orchid family (Orchidaceae) is a very large family (perhaps as many as 30,000 species) distributed primarily in the tropics. Orchid flowers are highly modified and distinctive, with **3 sepals** (1 usually modified) and **3 petals**. The **lower petal usually forms a lip** (sometimes inflated into a pouch), and it may also have a spur extending back from its base. Orchid fruits are usually 1-chambered capsules with many (often over 1,000) very small seeds.

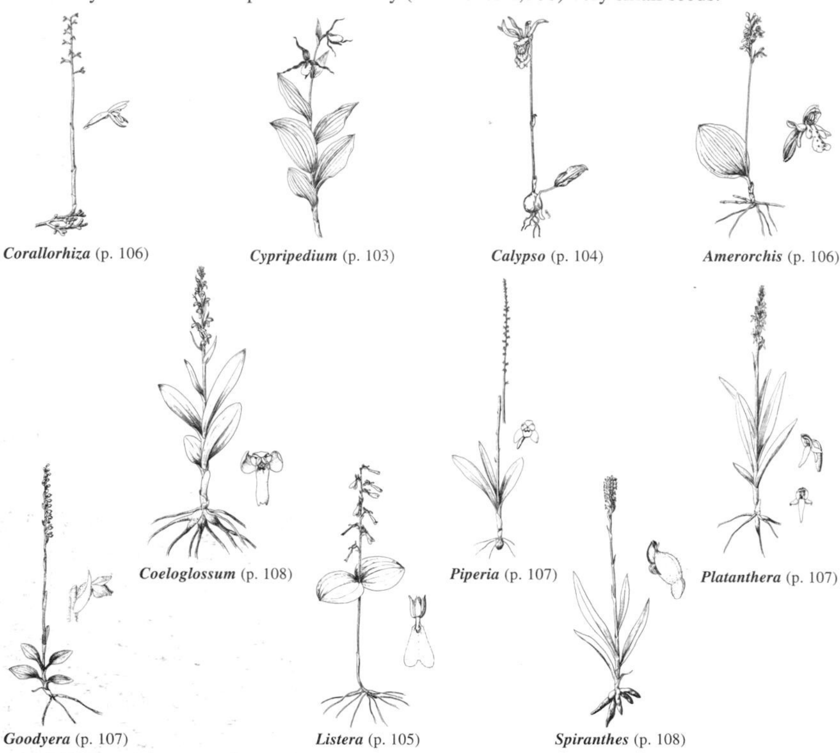

Corallorhiza (p. 106) ***Cypripedium*** (p. 103) ***Calypso*** (p. 104) ***Amerorchis*** (p. 106)

Coeloglossum (p. 108) ***Piperia*** (p. 107) ***Platanthera*** (p. 107)

Goodyera (p. 107) ***Listera*** (p. 105) ***Spiranthes*** (p. 108)

Key to Orchid Family (Orchidaceae) Genera

1a. Plants lacking green stems and leaves (saprophytic); stems yellow to reddish-brown or purplish; underground parts coral-like .... ***Corallorhiza*** (p. 106)

1b. Plants with green stems and leaves, though leaves may be withered by flowering time (not saprophytic); underground parts not coral-like 2

2a. Lower lip of flowers inflated, pouch-like 3

3a. Leaves 2 or more, basal or on flowering stems; flowers white to yellow .... ***Cypripedium*** (p. 103)

3b. Leaves single, basal; flowers pink to purple .... ***Calypso*** (p. 104)

2b. Lower lip of flowers not pouch-like 4

4a. Flowers with a spur projecting downwards from the base of the lower lip 5

5a. Flowers white to pale pink, spotted with purple .... ***Amerorchis*** (p. 106)

5b. Flowers white to green, not spotted 6

6a. Lip petal 3-lobed at tip; bracts much longer than flowers .... ***Coeloglossum*** .... (see *Platanthera*, p. 108)

6b. Lip petal not lobed at tip; bracts usually equal to or shorter than flowers 7

7a. Sepals 1-nerved; basal leaves usually withered at flowering time .... ***Piperia*** .... (see *Platanthera*, p. 107)

7b. Sepals 3-nerved; basal leaves green at flowering time .... ***Platanthera*** (p. 107)

4b. Flowers without spurs 8

8a. Flowering stems leafless; leaves in a basal rosette, dark green mottled or striped with white veins .... ***Goodyera*** (p. 107)

8b. Flowering stems with some leaves 9

9a. Leaves 2, opposite, egg-shaped to round, usually less than 5 cm long .... ***Listera*** (p. 105)

9b. Leaves several, alternate, oblong to linear; lower leaves more than 5 cm long .... ***Spiranthes*** (p. 108)

YELLOW LADY'S-SLIPPER
Cypripedium parviflorum

General: Sparsely glandular-hairy, perennial herb; **stems leafy**, 20–40 cm tall; from rhizomes.

Leaves: Alternate, lance- to egg-shaped, 5–15 cm long, sparsely hairy, with strong parallel veins, **slightly sheathing** stem.

Flowers: Mainly yellow, about 8–10 cm across, with **3 lance-shaped, yellowish to green, purple-striped tepals, spreading to top and sides, above an inflated (slipper-like), 2–6 cm long, yellow lower lip**, fragrant; solitary (rarely 2); May to July.

Fruits: Erect, glandular-hairy, ellipsoid capsules with 1,000s of tiny seeds.

Where Found: Moist to wet, shaded or open sites; plains to foothills; the Yukon and NWT to New Mexico.

Notes: This species has also been called ***C. calceolus***. • **Mountain lady's-slipper** (***C. montanum***) (lower photo) is similar to yellow lady's-slipper, but its flowers are usually borne in pairs and they have a white or purplish-tinged (rather than yellow) lower lip. It grows in dry to moist forests and thickets in foothills and montane zones from BC and southern Alberta to Wyoming. This rare, showy orchid is threatened with extinction in many areas, especially in the northern parts of its range. • Yellow lady's-slipper is widespread in the northern Rocky Mountains, but it is rare in the southern part of its range. • These beautiful orchids are declining in abundance near settled areas, because they are picked by unthinking passers-by and dug up by gardeners. Like most orchids, they depend on fungi in the soil for survival, making it difficult to transplant them successfully. They should not be removed from their natural habitat. If you would like to add lady's-slipper to your garden, some species are available in nurseries. Yellow lady's-slipper blooms after 2–3 years. • The gland-tipped hairs on these plants may **irritate sensitive skin**.

SPARROW'S-EGG LADY'S-SLIPPER
Cypripedium passerinum

General: Perennial herb, with **soft, sticky hairs**; stems leafy, 10–35 cm tall; from rhizomes.

Leaves: Alternate, **lance-shaped**, 5–15 cm long, with strong parallel veins, **slightly sheathing** stem.

Flowers: White with small, purple dots inside, about 3 cm wide, with a broad, green upper hood, 2 white, oblong wings and a white, inflated, 15 mm long, lower lip, fragrant; solitary (sometimes 2–3); June to July.

Fruits: Hairy, **erect, ellipsoid capsules**, 2–3 cm long, with 10,000–25,000 tiny seeds.

Where Found: Wet to moderately dry, open or shaded sites; foothills to montane; Alaska to Montana.

Notes: The gland-tipped hairs on the stems and leaves may **irritate sensitive skin**. • **Never pick these flowers.** They wilt quickly, and picking them kills the whole plant. • The 'slippers' are very smooth, inside and out, with the exception of a small section at the 'heel,' where there is a small, dense strip of long hairs. Bees and flies can enter the slipper easily through the hole at the top, but once inside, the only way out is to climb up the hairy strip at the back. Semi-transparent sections in the slipper wall let in light and help to guide insects to the exit. When they finally depart, the insects are first forced to pass the stigma, where they deposit any pollen they are carrying, and then one of the anthers, where they pick up a sticky mass of pollen to deliver to the next flower they visit.

VENUS'-SLIPPER; FAIRYSLIPPER
Calypso bulbosa

General: Perennial herb; **stems erect, 5–20 tall, delicate**, tinged pink or purple; from marble-sized, bulb-like corms, with thick, fleshy roots.

Leaves: Basal, single, dark green, broadly egg-shaped, 2–5 cm long, distinctly veined, wintergreen (develop in autumn and fade next summer).

Flowers: Rose-purple with purple streaks or spots and a tuft of yellow hairs on the pale lower lip, 15–20 mm long, with 5 slender petals and sepals, above a large, slipper-like lower lip, delicately sweet-scented, **nodding**; reproductive structure (column) purplish, hooded and petal-like, above throat of flower, with stigma near base and 1 sticky, 2-lobed anther at tip; **solitary**; late May to June.

Fruits: Erect, elliptic capsules, with 10,000–20,000 tiny seeds.

Where Found: Shaded, moist sites in coniferous forests; foothills to montane; the southern Yukon and NWT to Colorado.

Notes: These corms were used occasionally for food by native peoples. • This beautiful, little orchid has disappeared from many populated areas, because of picking, trampling, and digging. The delicate roots are easily damaged by even the slightest tug, so picking and trampling usually kills the plant. Transplanting rarely succeeds, because these plants depend for their survival on specific soil fungi that are not often found in gardens. Leave this delicate beauty where you find it, for others to enjoy. • Venus'-slipper is a good example of 'pollination by deception.' The flowers contain no nectar, and their pollen is inaccessible to visiting insects, but their colour and perfume mimic insect food flowers. Because Venus'-slippers bloom in early spring, they can fool naïve worker and queen bees on their early foraging flights. The colour, patterning and scent change with time and also vary greatly from one flower to the next, so a 'wronged' bumblebee is less likely to avoid the next Venus'-slipper it encounters. After a few fruitless visits, the bees learn to avoid these flowers, but by then they have cross-pollinated 1 or more of these beautiful orchids. • The genus name *Calypso* is the Greek word for 'concealment,' and these delicate little orchids are usually discovered in mossy, shady hideaways.

NORTHERN TWAYBLADE
Listera borealis

General: Perennial herb, glandular-hairy towards top; stems 4-sided, 5–25 cm tall; from fleshy roots.

Leaves: 1 pair, just above mid-stem, lance-shaped to elliptic, 1–5 cm long, blunt-tipped, stalkless.

Flowers: Pale to yellowish-green, about 1 cm wide and 1.5 cm long, with **5 small, slender, spreading upper tepals and a large (7–12 mm long), oblong, notched lower lip**; 3–15 in elongated clusters (racemes); June to July.

Fruits: Oval capsules, 4–5 mm long, with many seeds.

Where Found: Moist to wet, open or wooded sites; foothills to subalpine; Alaska to Colorado.

Notes: Broad-lipped twayblade (***L. convallarioides***) is similar to northern twayblade, but the 5 upper tepals are bent sharply backwards over the ovary, and the large lower lip is wedge-shaped (rather than oblong), flaring to 2 broad lobes at its tip. It grows in moist sites in foothills, montane and subalpine zones from BC and Alberta to Colorado. • The flowers of **western twayblade** (***L. caurina***) are smaller (about 1 cm long), with a wedge-shaped lower lip that is rounded at the tip (not notched or lobed) and smooth-edged (not fringed with fine hairs as in the other 2 species), with 2 tiny, slender teeth projecting from its base. This species grows on moist sites in montane and subalpine zones from BC and Alberta to Idaho and Montana. • When insects land on these flowers, they lick the nectar from a central furrow on the lip, beginning near the bottom. When the insect reaches the top and passes the stigma, a tiny drop of sticky fluid is put onto its forehead and a bundle of pollen (a pollinium) is stuck to the drop. The insect then flies off to another flower, carrying pollen to the next stigma.

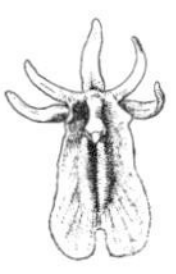

L. borealis

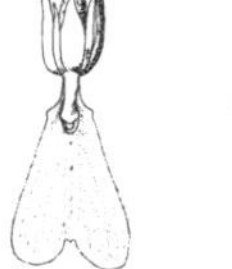

L. convallarioides

L. caurina

HEART-LEAVED TWAYBLADE
Listera cordata

General: Small, perennial herb; stems slender, **6–20 cm tall**; from slender, creeping rhizomes.

Leaves: 1 pair, near mid-stem, heart-shaped, about 2–2.5 cm long and wide, stalkless.

Flowers: Purplish to pale green, about 5 mm wide and 6 mm long, with 5 spreading, oblong tepals and a long, slender **lower lip split about halfway to base into 2 narrow lobes**; 5–16 in elongated clusters (racemes); June to August.

Fruits: Egg-shaped capsules, 4–6 mm long, with many tiny seeds.

Where Found: Moist to wet, usually shaded sites; foothills to subalpine; the Yukon and NWT to New Mexico.

Notes: This species has also been called ***L. nephrophylla***. • This inconspicuous, little orchid is widespread, but easily overlooked. • The intricate pollination mechanisms of the twayblades fascinated Charles Darwin, and he studied them intensively. The pollen of heart-leaved twayblade is blown out explosively within a drop of viscous fluid that glues the pollen bundle (pollinium) to unsuspecting insects. You can see this if you touch the tip of the column with a grass stalk or pencil tip. • The genus name *Listera* commemorates Dr. Martin Lister, an English naturalist (1638–1711). The species name *cordata* means 'heart-shaped,' in reference to the leaves.

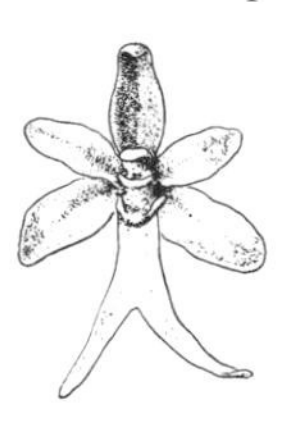

ROUND-LEAVED ORCHID
Amerorchis rotundifolia

General: Perennial herb; **stems single, 10–25 cm tall**; from thick rhizomes and fleshy roots.

Leaves: Basal, single, elliptic to round, 3–7 cm long, 2–5 cm wide.

Flowers: Pink to white, with purple-spots on lower lip, about **12–15 mm long**, with a small upper hood, 2 lance-elliptic wings and a broader, 3-lobed lower lip extended back in a slender, curved spur; 2–8 in elongated clusters (racemes); June to July.

Fruits: Erect, elliptic capsules, about 10–15 mm long, with over 1,000 tiny seeds.

Where Found: Moist to wet, shady sites; foothills to subalpine; Alaska to Wyoming.

Notes: This species has also been called ***Orchis rotundifolia***. • In Greek mythology, Orchis was the offspring of a nymph and satyr, which meant he was a creature of unbounded passion. When he attacked a priestess at a festival of Bacchus, the crowd fell upon him and tore him limb from limb. The gods refused to put him back together. Instead, they decided that since he had been such a nuisance in life, he should be a satisfaction in death, and they changed him into a beautiful flower—the orchid. • The roots of the orchid were once considered a strong aphrodisiac. Full, firm roots were said to provoke intense lust, while dry or withered roots would restrain unwanted passion. A drink made from these roots, called 'salep' or 'saloop,' was imported to England from Turkey and Italy in the 1700–1800s. In 1855, it was reported to be 'a favourite repast of porters, coal-heavers, and other hard-working men.' Old beliefs die hard, and the crowds frequenting the salep-houses were probably hoping for more than a relaxing nightcap.

SPOTTED CORALROOT
Corallorhiza maculata

General: Perennial, saprophytic herb, lacking chlorophyll; stems stout, **purplish or reddish to tan**, 20–50 cm tall; from **thick, branched, coral-like roots**.

Leaves: Reduced to thin, **semi-transparent sheaths** on stem.

Flowers: Reddish-purple to whitish, with red to purple spots on lip, about 1.5 cm wide, with 3 arching upper tepals, 2 spreading wings and a broader, wavy-edged lower lip with a small lobe on each side near its base; 10–40 in loose, elongated clusters (racemes); May to August.

Fruits: Hanging, oval capsules, 1.5–2 cm long, many-seeded.

Where Found: Moist to moderately dry, wooded sites; plains to montane; BC and Alberta to New Mexico.

Notes: Pale coralroot (*C. trifida*), also called **yellow coralroot**, is a smaller, more delicate species with small (less than 1 cm wide), pale yellowish or greenish (not spotted) flowers in slender clusters of 3–12. It grows in wet to dry, usually shaded sites in foothills and montane zones from Alaska to New Mexico. • **Striped coralroot** (*C. striata*) (lower photo) is a stout, robust species, 15–40 cm tall. Its large (about 2 cm wide), pink or yellowish-pink flowers have broad petals with 3 distinctive, red or purple stripes, and its lower lip has no basal lobes. Striped coralroot grows in forests in foothills and montane zones from BC and Alberta to New Mexico. • Coralroots are not green, because they have no chlorophyll (the pigment that most plants use to produce food). These plants are saprophytes, taking nutrients from dead organic matter through a cooperative (symbiotic) association with fungi in the organic litter on the forest floor. They cannot survive in habitats without the fungi, and they are rarely cultivated or transplanted successfully.

C. maculata

C. trifida

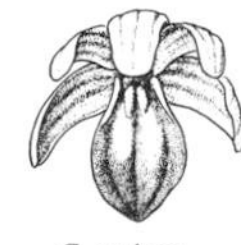

C. striata

WESTERN RATTLESNAKE-PLANTAIN
Goodyera oblongifolia

General: Evergreen, perennial herb; stems stiffly erect, 10–40 cm tall, glandular-hairy; from short, creeping rhizomes, sometimes forming large colonies.

Leaves: In a basal **rosette**, **dark green mottled or striped with white veins**, broadly lance-shaped, 3–8 cm long.

Flowers: White to greenish-white, with upper petals and sepal forming a **hood over lower lip petal**, about **1.5–2 cm long, downy-hairy**; petals 6–9 mm long; many flowers in 6–10 cm long, slender, spiralled or 1-sided clusters; July to September.

Fruits: Erect capsules, about 1 cm long.

Where Found: Dry to moist, shady sites in coniferous forests; foothills to montane; BC and Alberta to New Mexico.

Notes: The species includes ***G. decipens***. • **Lesser rattlesnake-plantain** (***G. repens***) is a smaller plant (10–15 cm tall), with 1–3 cm long leaves and 3–6 cm long flower clusters. It grows in moist to dry woods in foothills to montane zones from the Yukon and NWT to New Mexico. • The mottled leaf rosettes of rattlesnake-plantains are unmistakable. • Children once made 'balloons' by gently rubbing the leaves to separate the upper and lower sides and then blowing into them. These leave were also split open and placed, inner side down, on cuts and sores as a poultice. • Early settlers believed that because the leaves had scale-like markings, these plants should be used to treat rattlesnake bites—hence the name 'rattlesnake-plantain.'

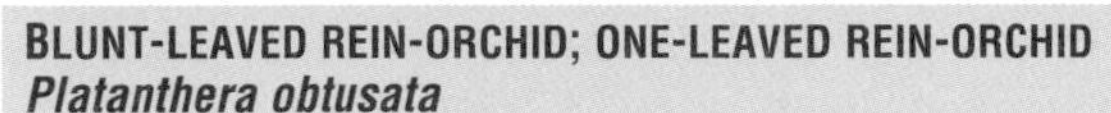

BLUNT-LEAVED REIN-ORCHID; ONE-LEAVED REIN-ORCHID
Platanthera obtusata

General: Perennial herb; stems **leafless**, usually 10–20 cm tall; from fleshy roots.

Leaves: Basal, 1 (rarely 2), **egg- to lance-shaped**, widest above middle, 4–12 cm long, blunt-tipped, tapered to base.

Flowers: Greenish-white to yellowish-green, about 1 cm long and 5–6 mm wide, with a rounded upper hood, 2 narrowly triangular wings, a long, slender lower lip and a similar, **hollow spur**; 3–12 in loose, elongated clusters (racemes); June to July.

Fruits: Ellipsoid capsules to 1 cm long, erect, with many tiny seeds.

Where Found: Moist to wet, wooded sites; foothills to subalpine; Alaska to Colorado.

Notes: This species has also been called ***Habenaria obtusata***. • Two similar orchids resemble blunt-leaved rein-orchid, but they are larger plants (20–50 cm tall), with 2 or more basal leaves. **Round-leaved rein-orchid** (***P. orbiculata***) (lower photo) has 2 thick, broadly elliptic to almost round leaves that spread on the ground at the base of its stems. Its flowers are fairly large (about 2 cm long), and their long (15–25 mm), slender, club-shaped spurs bend back sharply from the base. Round-leaved orchid grows in moist foothills and montane forests from the southern Yukon and NWT to Idaho and Montana. **Alaska rein-orchid** (***Piperia unalascensis***, also known as ***Platanthera unalascensis***) has 1–4 erect or spreading, lance-shaped leaves at its base, and its flowers are very small (about 4–5 mm wide), with broader (lance- to egg-shaped) tepals. It grows in moist foothills and montane woods and meadows, from BC and Alberta to Colorado. • Blunt-leaved rein-orchid is our smallest native rein-orchid, and mosquitoes (*Aedes* spp.) are its most important pollinators. It is not unusual to see a mosquito flying by with club-shaped pollen clusters stuck to its head like tiny, yellow horns. When a mosquito sips nectar through the mouth of the flower, the pollinia spring forwards and cement themselves to its head. When the mosquito visits the next flower, its head brushes past the stigma, and the pollen is transferred to that flower. To see this in action, simply poke a small twig under the hood of the flower and watch the pollinia spring down and cement themselves to the intruder.

TALL WHITE REIN-ORCHID
Platanthera dilatata

General: Perennial herb; stems **leafy, erect, 15–70 cm tall** (sometimes up to 120 cm); from fleshy, tuber-like roots.

Leaves: Alternate, oblong to lance-shaped, usually 4–10 cm long and 1–3 cm wide, gradually smaller upwards; bases sheathing stem.

Flowers: White to yellowish-white, sometimes greenish, **waxy**, about 1.5 cm across, with an upper hood, 2 wings, a lower, **broad-based lip** and a **slender, curved spur 1/2 to twice as long as the lip**, very **fragrant**; 5–30 in long, loose to dense, spike-like clusters (racemes); June to August.

Fruits: Erect, elliptic capsules.

Where Found: Wet, usually open sites in bogs, clearings and glades; foothills to alpine; the Yukon and NWT south to New Mexico.

Notes: This species has also been called ***Habenaria dilatata***. • Several other rein-orchids resemble tall white rein-orchid, but have unscented, greenish (sometimes tinged purple) flowers, whose lip petals are not expanded at the bases. **Northern green rein-orchid** (***P. hyperborea***, also known as ***H. hyperborea*** and ***Limnorchis viridiflora***) has dense spikes of flowers with long, slender spurs (as long as the lip). It grows in wet to moist, boggy foothills to subalpine zones from Alaska to New Mexico. **Slender rein-orchid** (***P. stricta***, also known as ***P. saccata***) has slender, more open flower clusters, and the spurs on its flowers are sac-like (saccate) and shorter than the lip. It grows in wet sites in foothills to montane zones from BC and southwestern Alberta to New Mexico. **Bracted orchid** (***Coeloglossum viride***, also known as ***H. viridis***) has a long, almost rectangular lower lip with 3 small lobes at its tip, and a tiny, sac-like spur that is usually hidden behind the petals. It grows in foothills and montane forests and grassy slopes from the Yukon and NWT to New Mexico. • The fragrant perfume of white rein-orchid is often smelled before the plant is seen. It has been described as a mixture of cloves, vanilla and mock-orange. Other common names include 'fragrant white rein-orchid' and 'scent-candle.'

P. hyperborea

P. stricta

C. viride

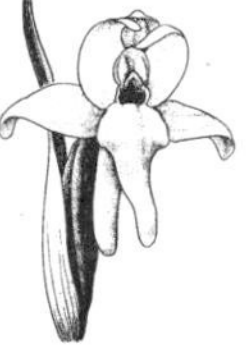
P. dilatata

HOODED LADIES'-TRESSES
Spiranthes romanzoffiana

General: Perennial herb; stems stout, **erect, 10–40 cm tall** (sometimes up to 60 cm); from clusters of large, **fleshy roots**.

Leaves: Alternate, **mainly near base of stem, lance-shaped**, 5–20 cm long, 5–10 mm wide, very small on upper stem.

Flowers: **White or creamy to greenish**, with an arching hood (of 2 petals and 3 sepals) above a smaller lower lip petal, 6–10 mm long, sweet-scented; many flowers in **1–4 vertical, spiralling rows**, forming **dense, 3–12 cm long clusters (racemes)**; June to August.

Fruits: Erect capsules, to 10 mm long, many-seeded.

Where Found: Moist to wet, usually open sites; plains to montane; Alaska to New Mexico.

Notes: Hooded ladies'-tresses might be confused with a rein-orchid (p. 107 & above), but the flowers of those species all have a spur projecting from the back of the lip petal, and their flowers are not spirally arranged. • These flowers have a strong, vanilla-like fragrance both day and night. The 2 pollinia are each 2-parted, and they split into delicate plates of granular pollen connected by elastic threads. • The spiralling spike of flowers was thought to resemble a neat braid of hair, hence the common name 'ladies'-tresses.' The genus name *Spiranthes*, from the Greek *speira*, 'a coil,' and *anthos*, 'a flower,' also refers to the arrangement of the flower cluster.

CARROT FAMILY (APIACEAE)

The carrot family (Apiaceae, also known as Umbelliferae) is a large family (nearly 3,000 species), mostly of the northern hemisphere. Carrot family plants are **usually perennial, aromatic herbs**. Their stems often have a large pith that shrivels at maturity, leaving the stem hollow between the joints. Their leaves are alternate, often growing from the stem base; they are usually compound, and the bases of their stalks usually sheathe the stem. Their flowers are numerous, in spreading or compact, simple or compound, **umbrella-shaped clusters called 'umbels.'** These umbels often have a set of bracts called the 'involucre' at their base. Their fruits, called 'schizocarps,' are dry and split in 2 when mature. Each 1-seeded half, or 'mericarp,' is flattened or rounded, and is often ribbed, winged or spiny.

Key to Carrot Family (Apiaceae) Genera

1a. Leaves undivided, lacking teeth, narrow .... ***Bupleurum*** (see *Zizia*, p. 114)

1b. Most leaves divided into leaflets or deeply cut 2

2a. Most leaves with well-defined leaflets, not cut into small, narrow segments 3

3a. Basal leaves undivided, heart-shaped, toothed .... ***Zizia*** (p. 114)

3b. Basal leaves, when well-developed, compound or deeply cut 4

4a. Leaflets 3, large (10–30 cm across) ...... ***Heracleum*** (p. 110)

4b. Leaflets usually more than 3, usually less than 10 cm across 5

5a. Leaves palmately deeply lobed or divided; fruits with hooked bristles .... ***Sanicula*** (p. 115)

5b. Leaves pinnately compound 6

6a. Plants perennial, from fibrous or fleshy-thickened, clustered roots 7

7a. Stem base thickened, hollow, with transverse partitions; some roots usually tuberous-thickened; leaf veins running to notches between teeth .... ***Cicuta*** (p. 111)

7b. Stem base without transverse partitions; roots not tuberous-thickened; veins not directed to notches between teeth .... ***Sium*** (p. 112)

6b. Plants biennial or perennial from taproots or stout vertical rhizomes 8

8a. Fruits strongly flattened, some ribs conspicuously winged ..... ***Angelica*** (p. 111)

8b. Fruits rounded in cross-section or only slightly flattened 9

9a. Leaves with well-defined leaflets; fruits linear to club-shaped, 8–22 mm long, not winged .... ***Osmorhiza*** (p. 114)

9b. Leaflets not always well defined; fruits oblong to rounded, 4–6 mm long, usually winged .... ***Ligusticum*** .... (see *Perideridia*, p. 112)

2b. Most leaves cut into small, narrow segments, without well-defined leaflets 10
  10a. Stems purple-spotted; robust, biennial weeds 0.5–3 m tall .... ***Conium*** (see *Cicuta*, p. 111)
  10b. Stems not purple-spotted; plants various 11
    11a. Plants with thickened, solitary or clustered roots .... ***Perideridia*** (p. 112)
    11b. Plants with distinctly elongated, sometimes fleshy-thickened taproots often surmounted by stout, branching stem bases 12
      12a. Fruits rounded in cross-section or only slightly flattened, usually less than 6 mm long .... ***Ligusticum*** (see *Perideridia*, p. 112)
      12a. Fruits distinctly flattened 13
        13a. Fruits ribbed above and below, winged at sides only ...... ***Lomatium*** (p. 113)
        13b. Fruits winged on upper and lower ribs, as well as on side ribs .... ***Pteryxia*** .... (see *Lomatium*, p. 113)

COW-PARSNIP
Heracleum maximum

General: Coarse, hairy, perennial herb, **1–2.5 m tall**, strong-smelling when mature; stems erect, single, hairy, hollow; from a stout taproot or clustered, fibrous roots.

Leaves: Alternate, compound; **leaflets 3, palmately lobed**, often maple-leaf–like, **10–30 cm wide**, variously lobed and toothed, hairy; upper leaves smaller and simpler; stalks inflated and winged at base.

Flowers: White, with 5 deeply lobed petals; outer flowers larger and showier than those near centre of cluster; many flowers **in twice-divided, flat-topped clusters (umbels), 10–30 cm across**, at stem tips and from upper leaf axils, with bracts at base of clusters soon dropped; late May to early July.

Fruits: Flattened, with 2 1-seeded halves (schizocarps), egg- to heart-shaped in outline, **7–12 mm long**, with a few vertical ribs and **2 broad wings**.

Where Found: Moist, open or shaded sites; plains to subalpine; Alaska to New Mexico.

Notes: This species has also been called ***H. lanatum*** and ***H. sphondylium***. • The **angelicas** (***Angelica*** **spp.**) are similar to cow-parsnip, but their leaves are usually pinnately compound with more than 3 leaflets, their petals are never 2-lobed, and their fruits are relatively small (3–8 mm long). One of the commonest species in the Rockies is **sharp-toothed angelica** (p. 111). It is recognized by its hairless fruits and its relatively large (leaflets 4–12 cm long), ascending leaves. • Cow-parsnip can be **confused** with its **poisonous relatives**, the water-hemlocks (p. 111). People with sensitive skin may react to the furanocoumarins in cow-parsnip, which can cause dark blotches, rashes and even blisters when contact with the plant is accompanied by exposure to sunlight. • Cow-parsnip was widely used by native peoples as a vegetable. Young stems were peeled, to remove the strong-smelling outer skin, and the mild, sweet inner stem was eaten raw or boiled. Unpeeled stems were sometimes roasted in hot coals. The roots were also used as a cooked vegetable, like parsnip. Toy flutes and whistles can be made from the dry, hollow stems, but these may irritate the lips.

WHITE ANGELICA; SHARP-TOOTHED ANGELICA
Angelica arguta

General: Robust, perennial herb; stems stout, **0.3–1 m tall** (sometimes up to 2 m), often ill-smelling; from taproots.

Leaves: Alternate, **twice-pinnately compound with lance- to egg-shaped, sharp-toothed leaflets** 4–12 cm long, hairless above; **veins directed to teeth or not reaching edges**; stalks inflated at base and clasping stem.

Flowers: White, tiny; in large, **flat-topped, compound clusters (umbels) of smaller, rounded clusters**, without involucral bracts; June to August.

Fruits: Flattened, elliptic seeds (schizocarps) with **2 broad wings**, 4–6 mm long, often reddish.

Where Found: Moist to wet, wooded to open sites; montane to subalpine; BC and Alberta to Utah and Wyoming.

Notes: Pinnate-leaved angelica (*A. pinnata*) is a more slender plant, with stems up to 90 cm tall and less complex (often once pinnate) leaves with narrower, more lance-shaped leaflets. It grows in moist sites in montane and subalpine zones from Montana to New Mexico. • **Dawson's angelica** (*A. dawsonii*) is identified by its yellowish (rather than white or pinkish) flowers in a single umbel from a whorl of large, leafy, sharply toothed bracts. It grows in moist woods and on riverbanks in the montane zone from southern BC and Alberta to Idaho and Montana. • Teas and extracts made from the roots and seeds of angelica have been used to aid digestion and relieve nausea and cramps. The leaves smell rather like parsley, and they have been used as a spice, garnish or vegetable. Stems of North American angelicas can be candied like those of European species. However, care must be taken not to confuse these plants with the **poisonous** water-hemlocks (below).

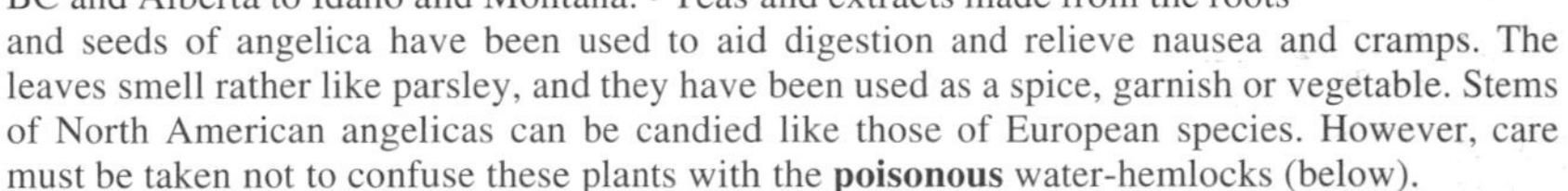

DOUGLAS' WATER-HEMLOCK
Cicuta douglasii

General: Robust, perennial herb, with **foul-smelling, oily, yellow sap**; stems erect, single or few, 0.5–2 m tall, thickened and **chambered at base**; from a taproot, often with clustered, tuberous roots.

Leaves: Alternate, 1–3 times divided in 3s; leaflets toothed, oblong to lance-shaped, 3–10 cm long; **side veins end at base of teeth**.

Flowers: White to greenish, tiny; **in twice-divided, rounded clusters (umbels) about 6–10 cm across**, with 18–28 main branches, with few or no bracts at base; June to August.

Fruits: Flattened, egg-shaped to round, 2–4 mm long, with **corky, thickened, unequal ribs**.

Where Found: Wet depressions, often in standing water; plains to subalpine; the southern Yukon and NWT to New Mexico.

Notes: Bulbous water-hemlock (*C. bulbifera*) is easily recognized by the narrow (0.5–4 mm wide), linear segments of its finely divided leaves and by the small bulblets in its leaf axils. It grows in wet sites from the Yukon and NWT to Montana. • **Poison-hemlock** (*Conium maculatum*) is another **deadly poisonous** species of this family. It is a large (0.5–3 m tall), freely branching plant with a stout taproot, purple-spotted stems and feathery leaves that are divided 3–4 times. It was introduced from Europe, but has spread as a weed to disturbed sites across North America. • CAUTION: All parts of these plants are **extremely poisonous**, and even small amounts can be deadly. Most native peoples recognized the water-hemlocks as violently poisonous, and some committed suicide by eating the root. The poison acts on the central nervous system, and it can take effect within 15 minutes of ingestion. Symptoms include salivation, tremors and violent convulsions. Even children making peashooters with the hollow stems have been poisoned.

C. bulbifera

HEMLOCK WATER-PARSNIP
Sium suave

General: Hairless, perennial herb; stems single, stout, hollow, solid at base, **strongly ridged, 50–100 cm tall**; from fibrous roots, sometimes with tuberous thickenings.

Leaves: Alternate, **pinnately divided into 5–17 leaflets**; leaflets lance-shaped to linear, 5–10 cm long, saw-toothed, main **side veins pointing towards tips of teeth**; submerged leaves more finely divided.

Flowers: White, tiny; in **twice-divided, flat-topped clusters** (umbels) 5–18 cm across, with 6–10 slender bracts at base; June to August.

Fruits: Oval to elliptic, somewhat flattened, 2–3 mm long, ribbed.

Where Found: Wet sites, often in shallow water; plains to montane; BC and Alberta to New Mexico.

Notes: Northern tribes gathered water-parsnip roots and ate them raw, roasted or fried. Although the stems and roots are edible, the flowerheads are believed to be **poisonous**. CAUTION: These plants have been **confused with the extremely poisonous water-hemlocks** (p. 111), with fatal results. Water-hemlocks are recognized by their twice- (rather than once-) divided leaves, their yellowish, strong-smelling (rather than white, sweet-smelling) roots, and their smooth (rather than ribbed) stems. If there is any question about the identity of a plant, consider it poisonous. Water-parsnips were collected in spring, before the leaves had grown; they had to be identified using their roots and the remnants of stems from the previous year.

GAIRDNER'S YAMPAH; INDIAN CARROT
Perideridia gairdneri

General: Slender, perennial herb, with a **caraway-like fragrance**; stems solitary, erect, 40–120 cm tall; from fleshy, **tuberous roots**.

Leaves: Alternate, usually **once-pinnately divided into long, slender segments** 2.5–15 cm long; often withered when flowers open.

Flowers: White, tiny; in **loose, twice-divided, flat-topped clusters** (umbels) 2.5–7 cm across; July to August.

Fruits: Brown, rounded, **about 2 mm long**, with several prominent ribs.

Where Found: Dry to moist, open or wooded sites; plains to montane; southern BC and Alberta to New Mexico.

Notes: This species has also been called ***P. montana***. • Another white-flowered member of the carrot family, **Canby's lovage** (***Ligusticum canbyi***), has fern-like leaves that are twice divided in 3s. Its stems grow from among a crown of stringy fibres on top of strong taproots. Its flowering and fruiting clusters are about 5–10 cm across, with winged, oblong, 4–5 mm long fruits. Canby's lovage grows on moist sites in open foothills and montane zones from southern BC to Idaho and Montana. • **Fern-leaved lovage** (***L. filicinum***) is a tall plant (60–100 cm) with leafy stems and large leaves (10–25 cm wide) that are finely cut into slender segments (1–3 mm wide). It grows on open or wooded slopes in foothills and montane zones from Montana and Idaho to Wyoming. • Yampah was an important food for many native peoples and mountain men. Some people claim that these roots are the best-tasting wild roots in the mountains, with a sweet, nutty flavour, devoid of any bitterness. They can be eaten raw, but usually they were boiled or roasted. Several tribes dried them for winter use, either whole or mashed and formed into cakes. The dried roots were soaked and boiled, or they were ground into meal and mixed with soup to make mush. • CAUTION: **Never** eat any plant in the carrot family unless you are sure of its identity. There are many **poisonous** species and experimentation is like playing 'herbal roulette.'

P. gairdneri